IF THERE IS A
GOD
WOULDN'T YOU WANT TO
KNOW HIM?

GUS BESS

DEDICATION

This book is dedicated to the glory of God and for the souls of men and women. Also, for my lifelong best friend and love of my life, my wife Karen, and our three children, Scott, Sandy and Danny.

"So whether you eat or drink or whatever you do, do it all for the glory of God. Do not cause anyone to stumble, whether Jews, Greeks or the church of God – even as I try to please everyone in every way. For I am not seeking my own good but the good of many, so that they may be saved. Follow my example, as I follow the example of Christ" (1 Corinthians 10:31 – 11:1 NIV).

CONTENTS

Acknowledgements..7

Introduction..9

Chapter 1: Born to Ride..13

Chapter 2: Haole Boy..17

Chapter 3: Paradise Lost..23

Chapter 4: The Windstorm..31

Chapter 5: A Home for Imperfect People..................39

Chapter 6: Join the Marines, Get a Tattoo................47

Chapter 7: Losing Larry Howard..............................55

Chapter 8: God on My Back....................................63

Chapter 9: Surrounded and Left for Dead................69

Chapter 10: Return of an Angry Man........................79

Chapter 11: Meeting Karen..89

Chapter 12: Back to Church......................................97

Chapter 13: Hungry for the Lord............................107

Chapter 14: Learning About God............................117

Chapter 15: A Small Change of Plans....................125

Chapter 16: Family Matters....................................133

Chapter 17: Undone..143

Chapter 18: Firsthand Restoration..........................153

Chapter 19: Knowing the Need Meeter..159

Chapter 20: Church Planting..167

Chapter 21: First Church of the Living Dead..............................177

Chapter 22: So You Want to Know the Lord..............................183

Chapter 23: A Draw to Holiness..189

Chapter 24: Never Graduate from Learning...............................195

Chapter 25: Israel and Ethiopia...205

Chapter 26: My Days in the Pit of Despair................................213

Chapter 27: Where in the World Is Post Falls............................221

Chapter 28: Embrace Your Opportunities..................................229

Chapter 29: The Church of My Dreams Was a Nightmare...........237

Chapter 30: Living Overwhelmed by Grace...............................245

Chapter 31: No One Like the Lord..253

ACKNOWLEDGEMENTS

I have so many people to be thankful for their encouragement, kindness and financial support for this book to come to fruition.

Dr. James and Sheryl (my sis) Major. Pastor Mike and Sandy Garman, Mark Maxwell, Wes Redding, Pastor Steve Calagna, Gary Del Giorgio, Tim Gidley, Charlie and Billie Potts, Chuck and Marianne Blevins, Mike and Carole Goodman, Don and Gwen MacLane, our Band of Brothers, some 140 men who meet at 6 a.m. to 7 a.m. every Wednesday morning for our men's mentorship, and First Baptist Church of Paso Robles, California, a congregation that has blessed me and my wife Karen these last eight years.

Then there is John Mason, author and speaker, who has been my mentor for writing this book. Without the help from him and his staff this book would never have come to be. And to all those people along my journey who have enriched my life in the grace of our Lord!

Thank you!

INTRODUCTION

What if there is a God? Could there be anything greater than knowing Him? Could He perhaps give you something greater than Himself? Is there a gift He could give to you that would be greater than Him, such as good health, an awesome reputation, beautiful relationships, or perhaps wealth beyond your imagination? I have asked this question to countless individuals, congregations, and classes at universities and seminaries.

For many people, thinking about God brings about the idea of some kind of a religion. Nothing could be further from the truth. All religions are somehow in the self-improvement program. That is not what God has in mind.

I have had the privilege of meeting many people who tell me they are atheists or agnostics. I tell them that I am sure that they are after the truth, and they always respond in the affirmative. So I make them this challenge: If they would be willing to meet with me for forty-five minutes concerning what is called "the Bible," and after that time if they were not convinced that it was true, I'd never bring it up again. But if they thought it could be true, I asked them to meet with me five more times.

Every single person who agreed to this ended up coming to know Jesus the Christ personally. To them, the words of John 3:16, 17 were no longer just some kind of statement. They experienced the love of God personally.

But it might surprise you to learn that atheists and agnostics who are far from God and tired, burned-out pastors have a lot in common. Many of the atheists and the agnostics I meet are honestly exhausted with the direction of their life. Careers are not turning out what they hoped for, many have had two or three marriages, and there is an ache in their soul they cannot see and that nothing seems to satisfy. They may not know they're looking for God, but they know deep within they're wishing for a change.

It may sound odd, but many who are in full-time ministry are desperate for a change, weighed down and burned out. They have been doing their best, but somehow that call to the Lord has been lost amid all the details in what is commonly called ministry. They're not in sin. They're utterly exhausted.

I often tell the story of living in Kansas City, Kansas, and meeting with a pastor who later became my friend. The Monday after the Sunday service, he asked me what I thought of his preaching. I said, "I don't know, I've never heard you preach." He was confused and reminded me that I was there Sunday. I told him, "I listened to a tired man talking. You're exhausted. It's not a sin to be exhausted. If you'd run two marathons back to back, you would be downright tired. You need to get a breath again." We'll come back to this story later, but the point I want to make is that this man was *tired*.

So many of us are. So what do we do? How do we get refreshment?

Everywhere I've been, whether I'm speaking to people who don't know Jesus yet or people who've been serving Him for years, they seem to experience God's grace afresh. I give to them what our Lord has put into my life: living Overwhelmed by His Grace. Regardless of culture or background, we need to experience the peace and joy that can come no other way than receiving and living in the free, unlimited grace that pours out to us through Jesus Christ.

Whether you're meeting Him for the first time or getting reacquainted after years of service, it is my hope that the stories of God's
grace in my life will renew and restore your desire to not just believe in
the Lord but to earnestly know Him. I want you to know that there is
no one like the Lord!

Second Timothy 3:16 NIV says, *"All Scripture is God-breathed...."*
That means every word in the Scriptures is His living breath. During
my life, I wanted His breath to become my breath; His Word to become
my word. I'm on a grand journey of learning to live that way, and I
want to invite you to join me and so many others who have received
new life by receiving the very breath of God.

If you entertain the possibility that there might be a God, know that
there is nothing greater than knowing Him. My hope is that no matter
who you are or where you have been, you may discover and be renewed
in the grace of the God who loves you!

CHAPTER 1:

BORN TO RIDE

People ask me how I got started. I answer that obviously, it began with my mom and dad! You've probably heard of someone who loves riding motorcycles so much that they've said they were born to ride. That's been much of my life.

When it was time for me to come into the world, my dad owned two vehicles: a dump truck and a 1947 Harley Davidson Knucklehead. (If you are familiar with Harleys, you will know that 1947 was the last year of the Knucklehead. In 1948, the Panhead was introduced.) When the contractions started, my mother told my dad, "I am not going to the hospital in a dump truck." So, she rode the Harley to the hospital and gave birth to me.

They named me William Trygve Bess. My dad was named Bill Bess, so they named me William so that I would not be a junior. Trygve is the name of my grandpa, my mom's dad, who was from Norway. But somehow the Swedish nurse who cleaned me up after I was born brought me back to my mother and said, "Here's Gus!" (If you know all the jokes that go on between Norwegians and Swedes, you have to see the sense of humor as to who gave me the name that stuck.) My parents liked it so well, I've been Gus ever since. When it was time to go home from the hospital, I did not go home with my parents in a dump truck. We went home on a 1947 Harley Davidson Knucklehead. Now, how cool is that!

When I was about two and a half years old, my mom gave birth to my little sister, Sheryl. Right away my mom started training me about being a big brother. I have always loved my sis and absolutely enjoyed being her big brother. It was during those early years my mom started teaching me that every young girl will grow up into a woman and some will become ladies because they are treated as such. So, she taught me manners from my youth to treat women with respect and honor so that they may know they are ladies.

We had a home in Reseda, California, and that's where I would be raised for the first eight years of my life. My parents did not attend church, although I do remember a couple of times my mom walked Sheryl and me to a small Lutheran church when I was five or six years old. The only thing I remember is how beautiful my mom was. She was beautiful from the top of her head down to her feet—a hat, gorgeous dress, gloves, nylons on her legs in those days and shoes that so complemented her feet. I was so proud to be her son.

I don't think my dad came. He had been a Marine in World War II, and he'd received seven Purple Hearts for his service as part of Colonel Carlson's Raiders. After the war, he became a detective with the Los Angeles Police Department and wasn't around much for my first eight years.

Like most kids, life for me was a lot about play, and then one day I had to go to school. But it started out hard since the teacher invariably saw my name was William and thought I must be a "Billy." She called for Billy, but I didn't know anyone named Billy; I was Gus. So, my first day in school, I was about to walk out the door with the teacher apparently yelling "Billy"! until she eventually smacked me on the top of my head. So, I learned to respond to "Billy" from people who really didn't know me. My family and friends always called me Gus.

However, things weren't good at home. My folks were having a very hard time in their marriage, and when my grandparents on my mother's side moved to Hawaii, they invited her to come live in Hawaii!—she gave my dad an ultimatum. She was moving to Hawaii with us kids, and if he wanted to stay married, he'd be moving to Oahu with us.

The miracle of miracles, he resigned from the LAPD, and we moved to Hawaii as a family.

Even though our family did not know the Lord, He already knew us and was beginning the preparations for a new future and a new hope for us all. Through all our opportunities, God was preparing us for something so good we could not have imagined it!

Jeremiah 29:11-13 says, *"For I know the plans I have for you," declares the LORD, "plans to prosper you and not to harm you, plans to give you hope and a future. Then you will call upon me and come and pray to me, and I will listen to you. You will seek me and find me when you seek me with all your heart"* (NIV).

CHAPTER 2:

HAOLE BOY

We lived on the windward side of Oahu in Lanikai and went to school in Kailua. From the fourth grade through the ninth, we lived in Hawaii. These were some formative years during which I didn't have to ever wear shoes, even to school until the 7th grade. In Hawaii I was what was known as a "haole." It's a derogatory name for a person who is not a native Hawaiian, especially a white person. That meant that I was going to get into some fights along my journey until I proved myself. In the sixth grade, I became a "hapahaole," which is a local boy who has been accepted yet isn't Hawaiian. I learned to speak the native language, which is a pidgin (a mixture of Hawaiian and English with a smattering of other languages for color).

Hawaii was a kid's ultimate adventure zone. I was very active, and I was willing to try anything. Climbing coconut trees, which make for some awesome forts, running on the beach, snorkeling, spear fishing, surfing—there was no limit to my adventures.

Once I found a parachute on the side of a mountain near our home in Lanikai. There was an air base on the other side of the mountain, from which I guessed the parachute came. But you may be able to imagine the uses a boy could come up with for his very own parachute!

I headed straight for the beach and the tallest coconut tree I could find. I gathered my parachute, climbed to the top, and prepared to float gently to earth.

It didn't quite work out that way. When I jumped out of the tree, I got reacquainted with the ground way too quickly and landed right on my back. It knocked the wind out of me, and for a while, I thought I was dead. Then the chute gently came down over me. (But luckily the next time I tried jumping with a parachute, as a Marine in Vietnam, thankfully it did open.)

No, despite my troubles (which I call "opportunities") for the first few years with the local kids, those years were good ones. My dad stopped drinking—he became an awesome dad. He coached our baseball team, was our scoutmaster in Boy Scouts, we built model airplanes to fly, and we shot rifles, shotguns, pistols, and revolvers. Life was awesome!

I would eventually understand my dad a lot better after my time in the Marines. I'll talk more about my dad later, but for now let's just say that fighting in World War II and then trying to come home again didn't work out magically on its own. In fact, the man who leaves for a war often is never the same person afterward. My dad was never the same, but the man he was while we were in Hawaii was different than the one he was in California.

I still remember the authentic luaus with the neighbors, where they'd dig a hole in the ground and put an entire pig in it to cook. We'd go to Lanikai beach, swim out and pull out some lobsters to boil in these fifty-gallon drums that had been cut in half. The whole neighborhood would turn out, music and singing would fill the air, and the women would dance the hula. (I also played the ukulele and wrote Hawaiian poetry that I'd give to my mom for her birthday.)

It was into this window of joy in our home when God began to overwhelm me with thoughts about Him. It all started while I was sitting on a pillbox one day looking at the ocean and the twin islands off Lanikai beach.

So, what is a pillbox? Some of you will envision that little thing you put your essential meds into. A few of you may picture something from an addiction story. I'm guessing relatively few will imagine the World War II-era pillbox I was sitting on in Lanikai, Hawaii, on a beautiful island day.

For those of you unfamiliar, during World War II they feared that the Japanese would invade Hawaii, so defensive points were built all over the islands. Just on the other side of the mountain where I lived was an air base (which provided me my parachute), and so they built these concrete bunkers from which you could shoot a machine gun through a narrow opening if our enemies invaded by the sea. They called them pillboxes, and I was sitting on top of one.

I didn't know any differently, so I was just talking to God out loud like you'd talk to a friend. I told Him, "You know, God, I think I've got Your favorite colors down—You're really into blues and greens." Around me were the vibrant green of the Hawaiian Islands, and all the different shades of blue from the ocean to the sky.

I was about thirteen years old then, so take that into consideration with what I said next: "You know, God, if You'd asked me to help You create all the fish in the sea, I don't think I could've come up with as many ideas as You did." I still am overwhelmed with joy every time I think of that. Something deep in me knew even then that God existed and that He enjoys our conversations with Him.

One day I missed the bus and so I had to walk home from school. It was only about three miles. It was on that day I noticed a church, which I found out was Catholic. Its front doors were open. This all happened just a couple of weeks or so after my conversation with God on the pillbox. When I saw the doors were open, I had a great desire to look inside but was absolutely terrified because I thought God would be in that building and would see me looking in and know that I was not one of His kids. I do not know where that thought came from, but it was spooky. But I so wanted to look in and get a glimpse of God that I snuck up to the doors in fear and looked in so fast that I did not see anything. Then I turned and ran! That night at home, I told my dad what I had done and then asked him, "What are churches?" He told me that night that churches did good things and were like the Rotary and Kiwanis clubs. He told me the only way you can go was to be asked by a member. That would impact my life for many years.

Christmas the following year, my mother gave me a gift—a real Bible. It was a Revised Standard Version. Looking back, I am sure she got it for me because I was so inquisitive about God. I really wasn't much of a reader, but I tried to read it to no avail. I did respect it, along with all my other bibles—the *Shooter's Bible*, the *Pistol Bible*, and the *Reloading Bible*. Even as a kid who knew nothing, I understood that what was called the Holy Bible was somehow God's book.

Whether you're reading this and thinking back wistfully to when things were simple and you were an innocent kid, or you remember when you first met God and had a childlike joy in your relationship, I want to leave you with something encouraging:

Innocence and childlikeness can be lost, but it can also be restored.

Our God is in the business of restoration. It's why Jesus came. It was God's focus while He was thinking and planning and prepping during the thousands of years between when Adam and Eve took a bite of that fruit that was forbidden and when Jesus stepped onto the scene.

Jesus is God's master plan. Quite simply, He changed everything.

Titus 3:3-6 says,

"Once we, too, were foolish and disobedient. We were misled and become slaves to many lusts and pleasures. Our lives were full of evil and envy, and we hated each other. But — when God our Savior revealed his kindness and love, he saved us, not because of the righteous things we had done, but because of his mercy. He washed away our sins, giving us a new birth and new life through the Holy Spirit. He generously poured out the Spirit upon us through Jesus Christ our Savior" (NLT).

I now know even as a kid that God wanted to meet with me. He wanted to talk with me and spend time with me, enjoying me like we enjoy spending time with our children. The thing is, He wants to spend time with you just as much! If you're open to Him, He wants to bless you with the best gift He has.

Himself.

CHAPTER 3:

PARADISE LOST

There's a season for everything, and even good things must come to an end. I'd earned my way up from a haole, to a hapahaole, which is an island boy who is not Hawaiian, but I didn't even understand the full extent of how Hawaiian I'd really become until we moved back to California. While my mom, my sis, and I loved it in Hawaii, my father really wanted us to finish high school in the continental United States so he moved us back to California.

Reacclimating to life in the States was hard for me, mostly because I missed all my friends and the culture I was so used to. An excellent example of how much I changed slapped me in the face when I went back to school and found that I couldn't even speak proper English.

While I hadn't been aware of it happening, on the islands I'd learned to speak the local pidgin, a potpourri of English and Hawaiian with a scattering of words borrowed from Samoan, Chinese, and other more exotic languages. (There is even a Hawaiian Pidgin Bible, which I happen to have a copy of.)

Tenth grade saw me not only trying to master the regular subjects in school but also learning to speak in ordinary English again! Even though I was born in California, it was like I was an immigrant trying to adapt to life in the United States.

You may recall that my dad had turned over a new leaf while in Hawaii and that those were really good years. Back in California, he morphed back into the old one, but while this was very tough for me, I now see that even in this God was doing something in my life.

My dad was a big man, very strong, and you may remember that he became an entirely different person if he took even a single drink. Well, he started drinking again, and when he did so, he could become angry very easily—and in that condition get physical. Down the street from our home was a small ten-acre ranch that boarded horses. Our two horses, Dixie (a quarter horse) and Laddy (a Morgan and thoroughbred mix) were boarded there along with eight other horses. Each horse had an acre fenced in, and I had the joy and privilege of being hired to take care of them all. I fed them at 5:30 a.m. and 5:30 p.m. every day, along with other duties such as unloading the alfalfa truck, mixing grain, and even (over time) learning how to shoe a horse.

A defining day came when I came home after feeding the horses to find that my dad had been drinking. To this day, I don't know what set him off, but when I came in the door, he punched me in the center of my chest and knocked me down. He picked me up and punched me again, knocking me down the hallway. He picked me up again to knock me into my bedroom, but this time I reached up and wrapped my hands around his huge wrist and yelled, "STOP!"

And, to my amazement, he did. He just stopped, turned, and walked down the hallway. I immediately shut my door, packed a suitcase, and went out my bedroom window. A friend of mine, Rick, came and picked me up. I knew his family well and even called his parents "mom" and "dad," and they said I could stay with them when I told them what had happened.

My dad had done this kind of thing before. In fact, in my senior year of high school he'd gone on these rampages being physical with me at least four or five times. But I'd had enough. I had just graduated high school, and this was *the last time* he was going to use me as his punching bag.

I had no idea exactly how transformational my time with Rick and his family would be. His sister, Pat, had married Kirk Jr., and God would use them to do some pretty incredible stuff in my life. But it started with water skiing.

Kirk and Pat asked Rick and me if we would like to go water skiing at Pine Flats Lake in the San Joaquin Valley for a couple of weeks and from there go up to Rogue River Oregon, where Kirk's parents lived.

It was then that my dad called me at Rick's house. He asked me to forgive him, and he promised he'd never do it again. He was genuinely repentant, and I went home immediately (and, by the way, he never did it again). But I still wanted to go water skiing and go to Oregon. At home, I asked my parents if it would be all right with them to go with Kirk, Pat, and Rick on this trip. To my joy, they said yes. We water skied every day for a week. It was a lot of fun, but we were exhausted after just seven days! So we decided to head to Oregon a week earlier than planned.

You see, I had an appointment to keep, though I didn't know it then; God had a major encounter with me planned up in Oregon, and the course of my life was about to change forever.

In Oregon, I got introduced to riding the rivers and to the green trees of the Oregon forests. I thought I'd died and gone to heaven, because while southern California is many things, green is typically not one of them. But up in Oregon, I figured I'd found out what heaven would look like on earth.

I got to pump gas for a few days for Kirk's father, Kirk Sr., at the Chevron station I think he owned. It's hard to put into words the enjoyment I felt being in Oregon, pumping gas, being in the woods, fishing in lakes and rivers and being around people who seemed to have a joy I did not understand. What more could a kid ask for?

It turns out, the answer is *logging!* I got to try my hand at logging with one of Kirk Sr.'s friends. His friend asked me if I would like to go logging with him, and I jumped at the opportunity! The next day, we headed into the woods, and he taught me how to drive a D8 caterpillar. We would chain up the logs and pull them up out of the ravines. It was every bit of a *WOW* experience for a teenager from California. I found out that working with my hands and running construction equipment was an adrenaline rush, and I thought that I wanted to live there and be a logger. But a bigger rush was waiting.

I was climbing off the cat that day when this logger (whose name I wish I could remember) asked me if I'd like to go to church with him on Sunday. Now, remember, I'd been taught that you could only go to church if you were invited, and in my whole life no one had asked me—until now! I wasn't shy about it; I was like, "Yes!" It was like I was finally getting asked to do something exclusive.

He wasn't expecting this kind of a reaction from someone like me, and he looked confused. He said, "Can I ask you something? Do you know the Lord? Do you believe in God?"

"Of course, I do," I replied quickly. "I'm an American! I'm not an African!" (Remember, I was seventeen and didn't know anything!) So then he asked me, "Have you ever been saved?"

Saved? Saved??? That question went over my head like the sound of an airplane going by. So I pondered his question and then I remembered something. I told him, "Yes, I've been saved." When I was fourteen, I was body surfing in Makapu, Hawaii, with my Uncle Lee, and I got caught in the undertow. It dragged me somewhere near three hundred yards under water—I was under for about two and a half minutes! But I could hold my breath for two minutes and thirty-six seconds, so I was just under my threshold when I popped up finally. My Uncle Lee swam out to me and brought me to shore. So, yes, I had been saved! I wasn't sure what that had to do with going to church, however.

So, he knew, even if I didn't, exactly how much I didn't know about church terms and customs when he brought me to church with him. It was a small Baptist church, and Kirk Sr. was a deacon there—whatever that was. After church I came back with more questions than ever.

However, at night, Kirk Sr. and I would talk. I would ask him questions about God, and he would answer me from his Bible, which looked very worn out. That following Wednesday, some kids my age asked if I wanted to come to a prayer meeting. I had no idea what that entailed. They explained that, while the adults met to pray, the kids went downstairs and played some games. When I heard this, I said, "Sure," but I should've asked what *kind* of games.

They were Bible games. The kids, twelve of us, sat around in a circle and asked each other *Bible* questions. And they weren't from the *Shooter's Bible* or a *Pistol Bible,* which I'd read; they were from the Holy Bible, which I had never read. I felt really awkward as they asked each other questions I didn't understand and provided answers I didn't know!

Finally, it came around to me. I was about to get really nervous. "Gus, here's your question," this guy said. "Who is the strongest man who's ever lived?"

I smiled at him and said, "I think I know who that is because I have seen the movie. It's either Hercules or Samson…." With that, a beautiful young lady sitting across from me began to mouth, "Saaaaamson." So I said, "I think it's Samson!" I didn't know these kids, but they suddenly broke out in this giant cheer when I said that. *Man,* I thought, *I really like this!* I was getting into it.

I'd survived my first "prayer meeting."

The following week, we did all kinds of things, but the most interesting was fighting a forest fire. The firefighters asked Kirk, Rick, and me if we'd be willing to help, and we said yes. So they gave all of us shovels and rakes, and we headed out to the fire.

I remember climbing up this mountain towards the fire where we were to remove the brush and the wind was blowing away from us. Then suddenly the wind changed, and the heat was like nothing I had ever felt. All at once, there was smoke beyond my imagination, and I remember trying to get out of there. The smoke literally sucked the breath out of my lungs. Then apparently I passed out and rolled down the mountainside.

When I woke up, I'd lost the shovel and the rake they gave me. I was in a narrow gully, and the smoke was like a solid ceiling eight inches above my face! By some miracle, I'd found the only clear air around; otherwise, I likely would've died. I turned over on my stomach and started crawling down—down and out of the smoke. It was nothing short of a miracle.

I look back at that time and I am amazed that God was looking out for me even then. When I knew *nothing*, His protective hand was on me. I could've died on that forested mountain, asphyxiated in the smoke, lost, and then burned to a crisp. But somehow, I made it out, and I now know God's hand was guiding me.

You may be like that right now—you may know nothing about God. You may think being "saved" involves lifeguards and not knowing Samson from Hercules. I've been there!

As a child, I'd felt drawn toward God, like there was a gentle current pulling me His direction. I'd talked to Him freely in Hawaii, feeling close to Him while surrounded by His creation.

But as I aged, the clarity of those younger days gave way to the confusion of *life*. Experiences got in the way. Life muddled up my view of the world and God.

Maybe you're like that right now. Maybe once upon a time, things were simple—or at least simpl*er*. But now they're complicated, and though you've learned a lot of things, you haven't learned how God feels about you.

Let me tell you the answer to that right now: He's crazy about you!

I know you have heard this: *"For God so loved the world that he gave his one and only Son, that whoever believes in him shall not perish but have eternal life. For God did not send his Son into the world to condemn the world, but to save the world through him"* (John 3:16-17 NIV).

He has His hand on you, like a father holding the back of a child while learning to ride a bike. Life is hard, and sometimes we fall, but our Father who loves us is right there, waiting to pick us up.

He's waiting for you to look His way, to turn around and lift your eyes up to Him. He's eager to make eye contact with you, and He doesn't care that you don't have your master's degree in Bible trivia.

He loves you with a radical love that will plunge through the roiling smoke in your life, pick you up, and go booking it down the mountain with a forest fire at your heels.

I experienced His goodness by *not dying* in the burning flames of an Oregon forest fire, but I was about to experience the kind of change that would take years to run its course, but it started with a bang. Or, should I say, a windstorm.

CHAPTER 4:

THE WINDSTORM

If you don't count a miraculously safe motorcycle ride to and from the hospital during my birth or not breaking my neck jumping out of a coconut palm tree to test a parachute, I had experienced my first miracle in an Oregon forest fire. The next week, I went to church with Kirk and his family again. I don't know how this happened, but Kirk and Rick got extreme poison oak from the forest fire, while I did not.

Somewhere around twenty-five to thirty people came to Kirk Sr.'s house after the Sunday evening service, and I found myself at the same dining room table where he and I would sit as I asked him questions about God.

(A little back story: the Thursday after the prayer meeting Kirk Sr. gave me a pink pamphlet labeled "The Gospel of John," and he told me, "This will help to answer your questions." So, I opened it up and found out that it was in King James translation, and I had no clue what that meant. I read John 1:1: "*In the beginning was the Word, and the Word was with God, and the Word was God.*" I tried to read on, but I couldn't understand a single thing. I read the first two or three verses over and over, trying to make heads or tails of it, but it might as well have been in another language!)

I don't remember all the questions that I asked Kirk Sr. around that dining room table, but eventually, I asked, "Well, where did God come from?"

He looked at me meaningfully and said, "That's easy, but that's not really what you want to know, is it?" As soon as he said that, everyone in the room got silent. I felt like every eyeball in the room was on me, and I became very uncomfortable! Kirk Sr. gently shook his head and smiled as he said, "What you really want is to know *Him!*"

Kirk (Jr.) rescued me, tapping me by the shoulder and leading me down the hallway into a bedroom. We sat down, and he asked me, "Gus, do you want to get saved?"

I asked, "What is that?"

"It's when you know God."

I started to feel scared and nervous, and I wasn't used to that feeling. I didn't get fearful and nervous, even when common sense should have made me nervous (such as going into a forest fire).

My mouth was dry as I asked, "If I did, what do I have to do?"

Kirk smiled at me. "All you need to do is pray."

"Then I can't be saved," I told him.

"Why?" he asked.

I was uncomfortable to say, "I've never prayed in my life. I don't know how."

Kirk smiled and laughed. "Gus, that's just a religious term for talking."

That was it? Then I had been doing it since I was a little boy! I'm good at talking, and I had at least a conversation with God on the pillbox.

I went to the window and knelt down, because in every movie I had ever seen, when people went to pray they got on their knees. I was so nervous! I can't even explain how overwhelming it was and how I actually felt.

I put my arms on the windowsill and held my hands in the way I had seen people holding their hands when they prayed in the movies, which felt very uncomfortable. I looked back at Kirk to see if it was okay if I interlaced my fingers as I prayed. He smiled encouragingly and let me know that was okay.

I took a deep breath, and then I looked up into the night sky. Suddenly I heard a voice so kindly say, "Who are you to look into the face of God?" Leaving my elbows on the windowsill, I bent over and prayed, "I'm not here to go to heaven. I'm not here to be saved, and I'm not here to be forgiven unless that's important to You. I found out it would be important to me. I'm here because I want to know You, and when this thing is over"—and by that, I meant my life—"I want to be wherever You are and to see You with my own eyes."

As I finished saying those words, I heard a sound like a sudden windstorm coming through a tunnel. It filled my ears, *whoosh!* Hit me right on top of the head, and went right through me! I could feel it from the top of my head right through my feet!

It scared me. I had no idea what had happened, and I burst into tears—tears of joy like I had never known. I looked over at Kirk, and he was sitting on the bed with his mouth hanging open, a look of total surprise on his face.

I asked him, "What was that?"

"I don't have a clue," he admitted.

"You should've told me that was going to happen! That scared the heebie jeebies out of me!" I said to him.

But my fear was completely gone, entirely replaced with a joy that I suddenly couldn't contain!

When I finally got myself together and wiped the tears from my face, we came out of the bedroom to find everybody waiting for me to come down the hallway. Kirk couldn't wait to tell everybody, "You're not going to believe what just happened to Gus!"

Kirk and I have never forgotten that day. He heard the wind just as I did, and it was a life-defining moment for both of us because he had never experienced such a move of God before.

The evidence of the change did not wait to show itself: I asked Kirk Sr. what I should do next, and he told me to read the Gospel of John three times as fast as I could. When everyone else went to ride dune buggies the next day, I told them I couldn't go because I was going to read the Gospel of John. They couldn't believe it, but I was completely serious. So I started again on verse one which says "*In the beginning was the Word, and the Word was with God, and the Word was God*" (KJV).

Everyone was getting ready to leave when I hit verse fourteen, which says that the Word (Jesus) became flesh (a human being) and came to live on earth. It said that we had seen His glory, and it was the glory of the only begotten Son of God. It was the same glory! Jesus was God's Son, but He was also God at the same time. I couldn't believe it!

I ran out to them and said, "Hold up! Rick, look at this; you're not going to believe it. I don't know how He pulls this off, but Jesus, the Son of God, is also God!"

Rick just smiled and shrugged. "Okay."

"No," I said. "How does that happen? He is with Him, He *is* Him, and then He became a *human being*? Jesus is God, but He's also the Son of God. How did He do it?"

Rick smiled the expression of someone who hasn't ever questioned how that could be true, and I went back to John.

I read the Gospel of John all that day. The next day they were going fishing, but I told them I wasn't going because I've got to read the

Gospel of John again. I read it the next day as well, so I had read it three times in three days.

Before my experience praying and feeling the very breath of God blow like wind straight through my body, I could not understand what John wrote. But suddenly it was as though something had uncovered my eyes and it was now crystal clear. I could read it as though it was in perfect modern English, but it was still the King James Version I was totally unfamiliar with. I was no master student to be able to figure it out intellectually; my spirit had come alive, and that was why I could now understand things of the Spirit of God.

We stayed in Oregon about another week and then headed home. I remember coming home and walking into my house. I hadn't told my parents anything about what had happened to me, and it didn't take ten minutes before my father figured out something had happened.

I told them about the waterskiing and what Oregon was like and the logging, but my dad suddenly looked at me and said, "What the hell happened to you up there? You look like my son, and you sound like my son, but you're not acting like my son!"

I didn't know what else to say, so I told him, "Dad, I met Jesus Christ up there." That's all I knew. I'm pretty sure I may have quoted something out of John.

I bought a Bible, and I just kept reading the Gospel of John over and over because no one had told me to read anything else. I knew there were other books in the Bible, but I didn't know I was supposed to read them yet, and no one had told me what to do next.

All I knew was that something had changed in me. Apparently it was easy to see, because even my father spotted it. I didn't have any conscious direction, but a significant shift had happened within me.

Perhaps you've been in a room where everybody's talking and then someone new walks in and the entire feel of the room full of people changes. Or maybe you've been outside right before a storm, and you felt the wind die down or change directions, just touching the tops of the trees, as the weight of a storm bears down. If so, you may understand how everything in life can change in an instant while at the same time seeming like nothing's actually happened.

Things were different within me. I couldn't put words to the difference, and I had no idea what it meant, but the course of my life had shifted. In a way, despite the wind that had rushed into me at Kirk Sr.'s house, the change was subtle at that point. I was the same person, yet I wasn't. Nothing was different, yet *everything* was different.

Does that make sense?

If you've never felt that, it may not, and that's okay. We can try to put words to our experiences, to describe them in eloquent detail and break them down into distinct points or steps. But all of it is a meager attempt to frame in human words something that happens at God's level, at a spiritual level. You won't get it until it happens!

I wasn't any different at a cellular level, my hair color was the same, I still liked In-N-Out Burgers, and even though I had not gone on the dune buggies or fishing, I still loved all the same things I had before. But I was *different*.

My spirit had been dead, but now it had come to life! I had been lost, but now I was found. I had been far from God, but I had just had an encounter with Him that left me changed from the inside out. If you've never felt like that, I am so excited for the day when your spirit, too, comes to new life in Jesus Christ! It's like nothing else in this world!

But it isn't about going to heaven. It isn't about being saved, and it's not about forgiveness. It's about knowing God.

Paul explains it like this: *"Therefore, if anyone is in Christ, he is a new creation; the old has gone, the new has come! All this is from God…"* (2 Corinthians 5:17-18 NIV 1984).

All the rest of that stuff follows. But it starts when your spirit comes alive and receives His Spirit. *That* is when we are changed; everything else is a by-product.

If you've experienced that but have forgotten that moment or lost sight of the forest in the trees, I urge you to sit back and ask God to remind you of that day. I pray that He brings back to your mind the feeling of being a new creation, of being made new. David prayed this: *"Restore to me the joy of your salvation and grant me a willing spirit, to sustain me"* (Psalm 51:12 NIV).

You may recall how I said that life had conspired to confuse the simple clarity of which I spoke to God as a child. That can happen after we're saved as well; we can lose sight of the life-changing miracle that makes us new and can become focused only on the trappings of religion.

When God touches us, it's genuine; when we make formulas about how to try to touch God, it's called religion. One has life; one is dead. God powers one, and the other is driven by our own efforts.

We can get sidetracked with things that are dead. When that happens, the essentials of our original experience connecting with God can become hazy, and our minds can become filled with all the things we think we are "supposed" to do and say to appear as though we are good Christians.

If that is you, if you're exhausted from trying to keep up the impression that you're a good Christian, I remind you of the same thing the person who doesn't know Christ needs to know: it's not about heaven, being saved, forgiveness, or any of the rest.

It's about knowing God.

"Create in me a pure heart, O God, and renew a steadfast spirit within me" (Psalm 51:10 NIV).

Set down all the trappings, all the distractions. Leave them behind, even just for a few minutes, and rest in the overwhelming grace that saves us. That grace is unchanging and is as powerful today as it was two thousand years ago. It is completely disconnected from your performance, and you do not need to earn it now or ever.

Take a deep breath, close your eyes, and simply thank God for His grace. He is here, with us, right now, waiting for you to know Him better.

Friend, it's *all* about knowing God.

CHAPTER 5:

A HOME FOR IMPERFECT PEOPLE

Have you ever been on a vacation you didn't want to end? I call them "mountaintop experiences." If you've ever had a perfect experience and not wanted to come home, then you may understand how I felt going back to regular life after coming home from my life-changing trip to Oregon.

Coming down from my mountaintop experiences in Oregon, I was about to be roughly introduced to a real-life fact many people pretend doesn't exist. It happened during my first church experience after being saved.

Rick asked if I wanted to come to his church and Sunday school with him, which was the invitation I'd been waiting for. (Remember, I didn't think I could go if I wasn't invited.) We'd been friends our last two years of high school, and I'd had no idea he went to church until going to Oregon. All that time together, and I'd never known, and he'd never asked me to come with him.

"What's Sunday school?" I asked. "What do they do?"

"They teach you the Bible," Rick answered.

"They teach you the Word of God?" I asked. It wasn't just "the Bible" to me—remember, we had other "bibles" in our home—but the words that God had written, *that* was different. If they were teaching God's Word, you could count me in!

Sunday rolled around, and we headed to his church. I had my new Bible in my hand, the Gospel of John well read but the rest an unknown. Sunday school was supposed to start at 10:00 a.m., but when we got there, nothing was happening. There was no class; everything was chaos. After spending an hour wondering what was going on, we headed into the main room where the service would be held.

Only nothing happened. Nobody did anything! People were wandering all over the place and talking, but it was nothing like I'd seen in Oregon. What was wrong with these people? What was wrong with this *church?*

Finally, around 11:20, this guy walked in, introduced himself as deacon somebody—whatever a "deacon" was—and announced that he had some bad news.

"Our pastor left," he announced. I wasn't exactly sure what a pastor was, but I figured he was the guy who usually did the talking on Sundays.

"Not only that," the guy went on, "but he took all the church's money with him." That sounded bad. "And deacon so-and-so's wife."

That sounded *really* bad.

I turned to Rick and said, "I feel really sorry for that pastor!"

"What?" he asked. "Why???"

"Because, if he knew the Jesus I knew, that woman and the money wouldn't have meant diddly-squat to him."

That was my first introduction to the fact that church people weren't any different than regular people—they can be just as dumb, just as driven by their impulses, and just as vulnerable to making bad decisions.

Individuals who look inside the church doors and see a lot of messed up people think that everyone in the church is a hypocrite—a fancy word for a person who says one thing but does another that even a lot of "unchurchy" people seem to know. They're more right than they may know, but the problem isn't that we're supposed to be better at hiding our faults; it's that we're to be letting people see how Jesus is getting into the middle of our messes with us.

Jesus knows that every single person who walks through a church door is a horrible failure and a sinner, a liar-cheater-stealer-hater and all the rest. He knew it when He reached out to us by leaving eternity as the Word and coming to earth as a man. It's not a surprise to Him that we have the failings we do. He gets it, and He is totally familiar with what it's like to be human because He *was one.*

Jesus didn't come for the perfect people (there aren't any). He came for the powerless, the lost, and the ungodly (that's all of us, even church people). That is why you find churches full of messed up, imperfect people. Paul tells us, *"You see, at just the right time, when we were still powerless, Christ died for the ungodly"* (Romans 5:6 NIV).

Even horrible situations can have a bright side. I never met that pastor who took the church's money and ran off with a deacon's wife. In fact, I never went to that church building again.

I did, however, go to its new location about eight months later when the church got a new pastor. Rick said his name was Allan Billington. "You'd like him," Rick told me.

He was right.

I liked Pastor Allan right away, and for some reason, the dude just really liked me and focused in on this know-nothing young guy who'd given his life to Jesus but had no idea what to do from there.

Pastor Allan was starting a Youth Department in the little, recently-troubled church, and since I was out of high school, I was open to meeting people. I went to the youth meetings about once a week, but I only showed to church ever so often.

Sometimes being at church was a little bit discomforting, because I did not know what to do or expect. But God was about to do something in me concerning my feelings about church. For instance, at the beginning of a service, everyone would get up and sing this song and I didn't know the words. I had no idea as to what they were doing. But when I heard it, I was so moved by the precious words that it made me, a young man of eighteen, burst into tears.

It was about *God*, and they were glorifying and honoring Him. It suddenly wasn't about me; it was about Him. My discomfort and feeling of unease just vanished as the focus shifted from me to God.

They sang the Doxology, and that shift was my first experience in true humility. It wasn't about me—it was about Him. It went something like this: *"Praise God, from whom all blessings flow; praise Him, all creatures here below; praise Him above, ye heavenly hosts; Praise Father, Son, and Holy Ghost, Amen!"*

I soon found out about "something Jesus the Christ wanted me to do." It was called baptism, and it involved being dunked under the water as a symbol that I'd left my old life behind and had taken up a new one, by the grace that I had received through Jesus Christ.

Pastor Allan told me, "It's a public statement of your faith, that Jesus Christ is your Lord. You're showing that who you were and what you are now are two different things. What you were, you are no longer. You're brand new. You're born again."

I knew that phrase, "born again," from the Gospel of John. Jesus told a Jewish teacher of His day named Nicodemus that you cannot be part of the Kingdom of God unless you are born again. Nicodemus didn't understand it; He asked Jesus, *"How can a man be born when he is old? Surely he cannot enter a second time into his mother's womb to be born"* (John 3:4 NIV 1984).

Jesus answered, *"I tell you the truth, no one can enter the kingdom of God unless he is born of water and the Spirit. Flesh gives birth to flesh, but the Spirit gives birth to spirit"* (John 3:5-6 NIV 1984).

Being baptized publicly declared that God had made me a new man in Jesus Christ and that I had been born again by the Holy Spirit.

I just hoped Pastor Allan wouldn't leave me under *too* long!

I had no idea getting baptized would be such a big deal, but it was—to my parents.

Pastor Allan made arrangements for me to be baptized, but it had to be at another church. Ironically, since it was a new location for the church, Valley View Baptist Church didn't have a *baptismal,* the place where you get, well, baptized.

I told my parents about it, expecting my mom to be excited. Instead, she was *ticked off!* I had no idea why.

I didn't have much expectation from my dad, but I was still surprised by his answer: "You can take all this Jesus stuff and stick it up your ———."

I was stunned. I thought at least my mom would be happy for me. She was always very loving. My dad's response wasn't all that startling, but the real disappointment was from my mom.

Not knowing why they were so opposed to my baptism, I went forward with it anyway. Even though I was saddened by my parents' response, I was so glad to publicly do something that showed and declared what God had done for me.

Pastor Allan and his wife, Nancy, were at the church where he'd arranged for me to be baptized. I was the only one getting baptized that day, and when he asked if my parents were coming, I told him I didn't think so.

With his wife Nancy watching, Pastor Allan and I got into the baptismal tank. "Gus," he asked, "do you have anything you want to say?"

I looked at Nancy and said, "Yes." I told her what Jesus had done in my life and declared with a loud voice, "There's no one like the Lord!"

Pastor Allan said, "Upon your public confession of Jesus Christ as your Lord, I baptize you, my brother, in the name of the Father, the Son, and the Holy Spirit. Buried in the likeness of His death, raised in the likeness of His resurrection!"

Then he dunked me. I came up out of the water with my arms straight up, celebrating like I'd scored a touchdown.

And as I cleared the water from my eyes, I looked over to see...my mom had walked into the room just in time to see me being baptized!

I was so excited! I couldn't believe it. I was so blessed that my mom had come!

I later found out my mom had baptized me as a baby in a Lutheran church. You see, people have taken Jesus' statements very literally (and lost their meaning along the way). She'd had me baptized as a baby thinking that if something happened to me without being baptized that I would go to heaven. You see, I'd been born with severely infected tonsils, and they were concerned that I may not live long.

But it hadn't meant anything to me as a baby; In fact, I had no memory or knowledge of it until I was an adult. When I made a public statement about my faith (even though it was just to three people), I was demonstrating I was a different person because I'd encountered Jesus.

But my infant baptism had meant something to my mom in her tradition of faith, and the fact that I wanted to get baptized again had at first hurt her—like saying what she'd done wasn't enough.

We worked it out. "You baptized me to know Him," I told her, "and I've always had this heart for God." I think a mother's love inspired her to take that step for her child and had an impact on my life. Years later as a seventeen-year-old I would take my own steps to affirm what she'd hoped for me all those years before.

Pastor Allan and I forged a lasting connection that would impact my life not just in those formative months after I came to know Jesus personally, but also because he became my mentor for the rest of his life—and what a mentor he was!

"Seek the LORD while he may be found; call on him while his is near. Let the wicked forsake his way and the evil man his thoughts. Let him turn to the LORD, and he will have mercy on him, and to our God, for he will freely pardon" (Isaiah 55:6-7 NIV 1984).

CHAPTER 6

JOIN THE MARINES, GET A TATTOO

I got baptized to declare that there is no one like the Lord—even though only three people were there—to publicly state that what happened to me in Jesus the Christ was real. I was passionate about God, and because I had filled up my heart and mind with so much of the Gospel of John, I was practically leaking the Gospel out of my pores!

That didn't keep me from being a teenager, however, and a fateful series of events propelled my life down an unexpected road. One evening, Rick and I piled three of our female friends, Sheryl (my sister), Patty, and another Cheryl into the back of my '55 pickup and headed for the beach. We took a favorite route—Topanga Canyon Boulevard, a fun serpentine road that curves through the wooded hills separating the valley in which I lived from the ocean.

I was driving. Topanga is a fun road, and I loved going fast through the canyon. The girl I liked, Sue, wasn't with us because she couldn't go that evening, so Rick and I were in the cab and the three girls were in the bed of the truck.

Well, it turns out I was going too fast, because as I passed a car in the canyon on a straightaway, I came to the next curve way too fast. We skidded sideways and rolled the truck! The girls were launched like torpedoes out of the bed, but amazingly they didn't even break a bone, though they were all still banged up pretty bad. Rick apparently put his hands on the ceiling of the truck as we rolled and somehow stayed in the truck. I, however, went right out through the windshield, fractured my skull, broke four ribs, and messed myself up royally. The other Cheryl, not my sis, had a head injury that caused her double vision for quite a few months. But thank the Lord, her vision returned to normal.

It's a miracle no one was killed! Topanga Canyon has steep sides, and the road clings to them in some places with a very sheer drop through a tangle of truck-destroying trees. If we'd gone over the side, everything would have reached a much harsher conclusion.

I spent the next few weeks recovering, and I was unable to do almost anything for myself. The four broken ribs were especially painful, and my skull fracture gave me headaches for which they couldn't give me any medicine.

Sue, the girl I liked at the time, was a beautiful cheerleader from Oregon, and she was a lifesaver. She came by every day for about two weeks and took care of me while my mom and dad were at work. Florence Nightingale herself couldn't have created a better setup; we were falling in love with each other. What guy wouldn't fall for the gorgeous Oregon girl who was nursing him back to health? It seemed like a match made in heaven.

But then something happened—my mother.

For some reason my mom didn't like Sue, and without telling me, she called Sue's parents and told them that they needed to keep us apart. The next thing I knew, Sue came over bawling her face off and saying that she had to move back to Oregon! Then she told me that my mom had called her folks.

I was so crushed and felt something I had never felt before towards my mom—anger. As soon as I was healthy enough, I enlisted in the Marine Corps.

Now, this may sound like a dramatic over-reaction, but I'd planned on enlisting in the Marine Corps my whole life because I wanted to experience war. In fact, when I was growing up I was afraid that by the time I could enlist all the wars would be over. As I look back, I laugh at my innocence, which was also my ignorance. Anyway, I loved history and most of it was about the wars of mankind. With my dad being a Marine fighting the Japanese in World War II, I hoped to follow in his steps. So when my mom had Sue leave our state, I decided to join the Marine Corps immediately.

I was a little anxious I wouldn't pass the physical, but I'd healed up well enough from the accident. I headed off to boot camp on October 7th, 1966—a bus from the Marine Corps Depot picked me up at San Diego airport. I was about to experience something I could have never imagined.

When we arrived at the depot, this good-looking Marine got onto the bus to greet us—khaki pants and shirt, ribbons on his chest, and smoky bear hat. He cut an excellent picture of a Marine. And then he began to talk…

He used words with a tone of voice I'd never heard before! We had just a few seconds to get our skinny butts off that bus and onto the yellow footprints countless other boots had stood on before us and after us. We didn't understand the realities of boot camp, so we were laughing and joking as we filed out—up until a drill instructor came up to one guy, asked him if he thought this was funny and *punched him in the gut!*

The drill instructor grabbed the kid by the collar and bodily dragged him into this building—we didn't know why or what would happen to him in there—and moments later they emerged with the kid's head shaved completely bald. I was about to find out that being a Marine was no laughing matter.

I had unbelievable emotions running through me. Fear, confusion, and something else that challenged me—and somehow, I knew that I loved it.

Boot camp was tough, but I really wanted it. They trained us, and I enjoyed working hard at it. I loved the obstacle course—I still do CrossFit training right now—and the eight or ten weeks seemed to fly by. My favorite story to tell, however, was snapping in at Camp Pendleton. For those who do not know what snapping in is, it is learning all the positions for shooting your rifle in combat. That is the initial training of becoming a Marine marksman.

Every Marine is a rifleman, and many people who sign up have never shot a weapon before—at least, not the right way. Well, while the rest of my fellow boots were snapping in, I had to go to the hospital for an infection! So, I missed snapping in, where they were teaching these tight firing positions. When I got out of the hospital a week later, I was called into Staff Sergeant Blue's office, our senior drill instructor. He was yelling at me that I had missed all last week's training, and he told me they were going to have to bump me back to another platoon because I'd missed snapping in.

"No sir," I answered precisely.

"Oh, you think you can shoot?" he asked me.

And I said, "Sir, I can outshoot you."

What I hadn't told him was that a Marine had been teaching me to shoot all my life—revolvers, pistols, shotguns, rifles, you name it. I'd won awards and had so many stories to tell. You see, my dad had been teaching me Marine shooting positions my entire life.

So, my drill instructor let me go out on that first day of really firing a rifle to see what I could do without the training the rest of my platoon received. As it turned out, I was the second-best marksman in my platoon. In fact, I qualified as an expert rifleman and thought someday maybe I could be a sniper.

I graduated from boot camp, together with Larry Howard, who would become my best friend, and we were given orders for our new occupation as Marines. We were both assigned MOS 2533, which is a radio operator. This would be our occupation going into Vietnam, so from boot camp, Larry and I went to radio school together in San Diego for six months.

This was so long ago; our first month was spent learning Morse code! In fact, we were the last class ever to have to learn Morse code. On weekends, Larry and I would drive up to the Los Angeles area to visit my folks, but during the entirety of my training, I was looking forward to going to Vietnam. Yes, I wanted to go!

After boot camp as a Marine private, one of the very first things I did was to get a tattoo. Larry helped me find it in this old tattoo store in San Diego; it was up in the corner of a wall of tattoos that had nothing to do with the military. It was an old World War I tattoo, and it cost me thirteen dollars.

We immediately hopped into my truck and drove 150 miles north to my folks' place. I probably really scared my mom by knocking on the door at 2:00 a.m., and she was very surprised to see us at her door at that hour. I walked past her to get my dad, and when he came out, his face looked confused as to why we were there at his house at 2:00 in the morning.

Then I pulled off my shirt.

My dad had always told me not to get a tattoo, but as I pulled the bandages off my right shoulder and showed him, he said, "No you didn't... Well, if you had to get one, you got a good one!"

It was the same tattoo he had—same shoulder, same place. I was pumped!

Even after all my conditioning in boot camp, my dad was still a huge man to me, and the look I saw in his eyes that night is something I'll never forget.

We never know the course our lives take. If my dad's drinking and violence had not driven me out of the house as a teenager, I don't know if I would've ever gone to Oregon and gotten to know Kirk Sr. or Kirk Jr. as well. Would I have come to know Jesus? Would I have had the same experience of the rushing wind? I don't know. If I had not been in a car wreck, would Sue and I have gotten so close that my mom would call her parents? Would I have still enlisted in the Marines? I don't know that either.

I also don't know what types of bad things you may have gone through. They may weigh heavily on your soul or seem like scars on your life that serve as daily reminders of the difficult times you've survived.

I never want to downplay the hurts people go through because they are very real and impact our lives profoundly. However, in my life, I have seen that even though I have gone through very dark times, the mere fact I can talk about them and write about them means I made it through. I may be scarred, but I'm still alive.

In fact, I have seen God's goodness with my own eyes. Because no matter what I went through, He was kind enough to bring me through and even turn my painful experiences around.

You see, God is good—*all good*. He is so good that He can bring good out of everything. Does that mean that God brings everything, even bad things, into our lives so He can turn them to good? I don't believe so—He gives good gifts to His kids. He brings goodness with Him, and when we welcome Him into our lives and problems, goodness and grace come with Him to take up residence in our lives. They go to work, like remodelers. God is the remodeler of broken lives.

The Bible tells us, *"We know that God causes everything to work together for the good of those who love God and are called according to his purpose for them"* (Romans 8:28 NLT). Notice, it doesn't say that He causes all things, but He causes all things to work for the good of those who love God.

James goes so far as to say, *"Dear brothers and sisters, when troubles come your way, consider it an opportunity for great joy. For you know that when your faith is tested, your endurance has a chance to grow. So let it grow, for when your endurance is fully developed, you will be perfect and complete, needing nothing"* (James 1:2-4 NLT).

The next time something bad comes your way, I challenge you to do this: keep your eyes open. Be watching, because troubles are chances to see God at work. Your difficulty is an opportunity, so pay attention to what God will do with it.

It may take weeks, months, or even years, but I guarantee that in your life of love for God, He is working something good. He takes the wrong and evil things this world and its master throws at us, and He begins working them for our good.

Need some good in your bad situation? Invite God in, give Him space to operate, and watch what He does.

You won't be disappointed.

CHAPTER 7:

LOSING
LARRY HOWARD

Larry Howard and I really became best friends in radio school. We both trained to be radio operators in the United States Marine Corps, and we spent about six months in San Diego, 150 miles from home for me. Larry was from Illinois, so on weekends, we would go visit my family.

At this point, I was still reading the Gospel of John—so much so that it just leaked out of me. Eventually, someone told me I could read other books of the Bible, too. So I started reading Acts, the book that follows John in the Bible. As I read Acts, I came to the part where during this celebration called Pentecost the Holy Spirit came to those who had gathered together awaiting the fulfillment of a promise Jesus had made to them.

Jesus spent forty days with His disciples after He defeated death, hell, and the grave and before He went up to heaven. He told them this:

"Do not leave Jerusalem until the Father sends you the gift he promised, as I told you before. John baptized with water, but in just a few days you will be baptized with the Holy Spirit...You will receive power when the Holy Spirit comes upon you. And you will be my witnesses, telling people about me everywhere—

in Jerusalem, throughout Judea, in Samaria, and to the ends of the earth" (Acts 1:4-5,8 NLT).

When He told them to stay in Jerusalem because He would rise from the dead, they didn't listen to Him. When the resurrected Jesus stood before them with nail holes in His hands and feet and a spear wound in His side, they took His instructions seriously. They waited for the promise, and we read,

"On the day of Pentecost all the believers were meeting together in one place. Suddenly, there was a sound from heaven like the roaring of a mighty windstorm, and it filled the house where they were sitting. Then, what looked like flames or tongues of fire appeared and settled on each of them. And everyone present was filled with the Holy Spirit and began speaking in other languages, as the Holy Spirit gave them this ability" (Acts 2:1-4 NLT).

When I saw this, it simply blew me away. I had never heard of anything like the experience I had in front of the window with Kirk when I prayed and accepted Jesus. I knew that I had felt that same wind! At first, I had just assumed everyone had an experience like this, but I had since learned that this was not what happened when everyone got saved. I knew exactly what had occurred in the upper room where the disciples had gathered because that was exactly what happened to me!

However, I next noticed the fire thing—that hadn't happened to me. I only had the wind. I didn't know anything about the Holy Spirit, but if that was part of their experience I wanted to know more.

I would, but not right away—first, I had to go through a detour through hell.

Larry was around me as the Gospel of John oozed out of my pores. I often shared John with him and showed him the things I had learned in the Word of God. I took him to church with me a few times on Sundays, but it wasn't until we had driven up to the top of a mountain and were sitting together, eating sandwiches and drinking Budweiser beer while reading the Gospel of John, that I asked Larry if he wanted to know the Jesus I knew.

Larry prayed this simple prayer to Jesus: "I want to receive Your grace, and I want to know You. I confess on this day that Jesus Christ is my Savior and Lord."

The love of God was real to him, too, but all this Christian stuff was brand-new to both of us! We happily sat together and enjoyed the view while eating our sandwiches, drinking our beers, and memorizing both the preamble on the Budweiser cans and the beginning of the Gospel of John!

Two weeks later, I told Pastor Allan that Larry had gotten saved, and since the church now had a baptistery, Larry went forward one morning and was baptized. We were both full of so much joy! It was an incredibly exciting time because I could share my passionate experience with God with my dearest friend. I was having a blast!

Two and a half months later, we graduated from radio school and got our orders. I was disappointed to find that I was being sent to Camp Lejeune, North Carolina. Larry was headed to Vietnam.

The thing was, I wanted to go to Vietnam, and Larry didn't. We went to our commanding officer and asked if our orders could be flipped. We were almost the same Marine—we had the same qualifications, and we had both just graduated and made Private First Class. Couldn't we just trade?

But it doesn't work that way. We both went on leave for fifteen days, and Larry went back to Illinois to be with his family. He came back to California and stayed at my folks' house for a while, but then it was time for us both to go. I would be flying to North Carolina, and Larry would be headed for Vietnam.

Being very emotional, I gave him a hug, shook his hand, and said, "Larry, Jesus Christ is with you! Don't worry about it. Go kick some butt, and I'll see you in thirteen months."

It was the last time I saw Larry Howard.

He was in Vietnam sixteen days when he was killed.

When I arrived in Camp Lejeune, they asked us if anyone wanted to be airborne. My hand went up right away! They put me in an outfit called 2nd ANGLCO. It was an Air Naval Gunfire Liaison Company, which was airborne Marines. Three days later, I was on a plane to Guantanamo Bay, Cuba. My Marine Company would be there for six months, and it was there I would go through Junior Jump School, getting ready for jump school at Fort Benning, Georgia. I was in Cuba just a few days when I got a letter from my dad saying that Larry had been killed.

I went to my rack—what the Marines call a bunk or a bed—and I wailed! I cried and cried like I never had before. They wouldn't let me go to the funeral; I wasn't a blood relative. It turns out being in Cuba was a good thing, because I would've gone AWOL to go if I could've, but I couldn't swim to Florida.

I was so angry with the Lord! I swore at Him and told Him what a lousy God He was because He couldn't even keep Larry alive. I told Him I would never serve Him again and to leave me alone from now on.

Even though I was about to make some very bad choices, you will see that the Lord did not leave me alone.

I was moving forward, with my training and my grief, but not necessarily the right direction. I wanted to go to Vietnam more than ever now, and I wrote requests regularly. They kept turning me down! I also started drinking. I'd bet people a beer that I could jump off a two- or three-story building and not get hurt. You just can't jump straight down, you've got to be moving forward, I told them. (By the way, it was a dumb way to get beer, especially then, because they were only 10 cents. I did not say I was brilliant.)

I headed back to the States for jump school, and the first thing they taught us was how to fall. Depending on which way the wind is blowing, they wanted you to fall frontwards or backward or to the side. They started school by teaching us how to do a parachute landing fall, which we know as a PLF. Next was being harnessed into a parachute, then lifted into a 250-foot tall tower where we would be released to practice our PLF.

Let me just say that the adrenaline rush of jumping out of an airplane can be therapeutic. My first jump was incredible. They say most people shut their eyes when they come out of the airplane, but I was determined I wouldn't close my eyes. I was to be the first man out of the flying boxcar we went up in, and as I put my hands on the outside of the airplane and squatted down, I was amazed by the view. It was like a dream. Just when I was about to jump, suddenly someone hit me on the butt—hard!

I was out of the airplane, turning as the wind hit me. *"Geronimo!"* I yelled.

I kept my eyes open the whole time, watching my feet and the horizon and then my feet and the earth. Looking up at the open chute was overwhelming joy! My first landing was just plain exciting. As I got to my feet and looked up at where I'd been, I couldn't believe I was getting to do this.

We did that every day for five days—the same location but under different circumstances. On our third jump it was a very windy day, they almost canceled; a lot of guys broke their legs that day because they stiffened up just moments before they hit the ground, instead of landing with the flexibility of a drunk. I remember hearing one guy's leg crack like a breaking tree limb! But, like I said, I was good at falling. We did five jumps, but I wanted to do ten so I could get my Marine gold wings!

I loved jump school, but bitterness at God for letting Larry get killed was eating me up inside, and I was making poor decisions.

Once a buddy of mine and I went on what we called the swoop from North Carolina to Washington, D.C. We'd go up for the weekend, and since my friend Danny had never been, I wanted to show him around.

We'd been taking in the sights and doing some drinking, and we headed back to the YMCA where we were staying for two dollars a night. Danny was quite intoxicated, and I was trying my best to get him back to the Y. As we were walking, we found ourselves in what ended up as a bad part of town for two Marines.

Six men with knives came out of nowhere and surrounded us. Danny was plastered, but I figured I was trained, in fantastic shape, and feeling angry with the men trying to rob me. They demanded our money, and I told them, "Guys, do yourselves a favor. Put your knives away, or I will stick them up your ass!" And with that, they all backed off, and I thought that was cool!

No sooner did they back off than up pulled a police car—which they had of course seen coming! The officers asked if we needed a ride, but I didn't want Danny to get arrested, so I said we didn't! They asked me if I knew where I was and I told them I did. I was in the capitol of the greatest country on earth, the Untitled States of America. They said, "Okay," and then drove off. So we crossed the street and began walking. I noticed the six men were now following us, and then we crossed a major intersection, which seemed to be an invisible border, and the six men turned back to their neighborhood. When I think back, even then the Lord watched out for me and Danny, for it was a miracle that we did not get knifed and robbed.

I know now that God was looking out for me, even when I was angry with Him.

Another time, while I was still in jump school in Georgia, I was in line to make a phone call back to my parents. There was only one pay phone booth—if you can remember those—and I was standing in line with dozens of Army dudes to make a call.

I was talking to a guy from the Army in front of me, and he was waiting to call his wife back in New York. We got through the whole line, and finally, it was this guy's turn. He was in the middle of his call when this huge black man, Army Spec 4, walked up and just grabbed and pulled him out of the phone booth!

"I want to make a call," he rumbled.

By this point, I was the only one left in line. And I thought, *Who does this guy think he is?* I grabbed him by his shirt on his right shoulder and pulled him out of the booth and said, "He's been waiting in line for an hour to call his wife, so you get to the end of the line!" Then I said, "And by the way, I'm the end of the line."

Suddenly, someone behind me grabbed my arms and pulled them back. The huge dude I'd grabbed started to throw a punch, but I used the guy holding my arms as leverage and lifted both legs to kick. I got him in the chest, and he went sprawling backward onto his rear!

Suddenly, three or four other guys were all trying to hit me, and I still couldn't get my arms loose. But somehow, not *one* of them landed a punch. The next thing I knew, the MPs were there, and we all ran into a nearby NCO club. The MPs came storming in, demanding to know who was out there, but suddenly "nobody knows *nothing*"! All at once, it just looked like everybody liked each other.

I never did get to make that phone call.

You may be mad at God right now. Many people are, and it can feel like you've got a pretty good reason! The odd thing is that many of us are afraid to admit it.

As if He doesn't already know!

We blame Him for doing things or not doing things. We wish things were different. The miracle we hoped for never happened, so we are just plain mad at God.

My bitterness and anger led me down dark paths, consuming my joy and robbing me of the goodness and light that had been part of my days since I had received God's wonderful gift of grace in Jesus the

Christ. The freedom and hope that I'd known were washed under waves of grief and anger and bitterness.

Perhaps you can identify. Maybe things used to be better, brighter, or clearer before some tragedy or difficult event came into your life. Perhaps in your anger, you've forgotten God, or you're all too aware of Him but too angry to speak to Him.

I want to encourage you with something: No matter how you feel about God, how He feels about you hasn't changed.

He still loves you with a never-ending, never giving up, always and forever love. It never fades, and it's as bright and fresh today as it was the day you were born and the day you were born *again*.

Paul had this to say about the nature of God's love:

"Can anything ever separate us from Christ's love? Does it mean he no longer loves us if we have trouble or calamity, or are persecuted, or hungry, or destitute, or in danger, or threatened with death? (As the Scriptures say, 'For your sake we are killed every day; we are being slaughtered like sheep.') No, despite all these things, over-whelming victory is ours through Christ, who loved us. And I am convinced that nothing can ever separate us from God's love. Neither death nor life, neither angels nor demons, neither our fears for today nor our worries about tomorrow—not even the powers of hell can separate us from God's love. No power in the sky above or in the earth below—indeed, nothing in all creation will ever be able to separate us from the love of God that is revealed in Christ Jesus our Lord" (Romans 8:35-39 NLT).

While I suffered grief after Larry's death and wanted nothing to do with God, His grace and love never left me. The power to forgive and be renewed was within me, though I did not recognize it. Even when I wanted nothing to do with Him, He was with me, and I could feel His presence.

CHAPTER 8:

GOD ON MY BACK

I was very hurt that God hadn't kept Larry alive, and in my anger, I told Him to take a hike. I didn't want anything more to do with Him.

But He wouldn't listen to me or get off my back. I could feel His presence all the time! It was infuriating—to the point that I would sometimes turn, look at my left shoulder, and whisper, "Get off my back!" to Him.

But He wouldn't go! He followed me through jump school and back to Camp Lejeune, where the First Sergeant said, "Bess, pack your things. You got your request—you're going to 'Nam."

After a short leave, I flew first to Okinawa and from there to Da Nang, Vietnam. It was the first of May, 1968. I walked off the plane into Vietnam's cloying, humid heat unsure of what to do or where I'd be going. Suddenly, I heard my voice being called. "Bess and Singer, you guys are going to First Recon Battalion."

"Cool," I answered. Singer, a Jewish guy, and I were both radio operators, and I quickly learned that the first two people shot on a patrol when being attacked were the lieutenant, who was the patrol leader, and the primary radio operator which was me.

Not cool.

They assigned me a hooch, the building I'd be living in. It was a plywood building with screen sides and a tin roof. Many times, we used diesel fuel to mop the floor because it kept the bugs out. Eventually, you got used to the smell, but the bugs didn't.

I found my rack, my body trying to figure out what time zone it was in, and fell asleep. But I was suddenly woken up. Some of the meanest people on the planet had invaded the hooch and were intent on initiating me to Recon in Vietnam!

They were Recon Marines, and I'd unwittingly become the centerpiece of an initiation.

You see, only seven Marines would go into the jungle for ten to fourteen days at a time on recon missions, and no matter what—if you got shot, hit by shrapnel, or took a pongee stick through your foot—*no matter what*, you could not make a sound. If you did, the enemy—and there were way more than seven of them—could find you, kill you, or capture and torture you along with your fellow Marines.

So, in Recon, there was an initiation—I didn't know a thing about it—and they wanted to see if you were going to make a lot of noise and get them all killed. They ripped off my shirt, put a gag in my mouth, and hissed at me to shut up. Suddenly one of them bit my left shoulder!

"Don't make a sound," one guy told me.

Another bit me on the upper part of my right arm! In fact, he bit my arm so badly he tore a piece of flesh right off the back of my arm and *ate it* right in front of me!

And these were the guys on *my side!* This wasn't even the enemy yet!

The guy who bit me, I found out, was a supply sergeant. He'd been in Vietnam for thirty months, and he'd seen too much combat. It messed something up inside of him.

In fact, he was so toxic my arm got infected from his crazy bite! It swelled up as big as my leg, which posed a problem. I went to the medics, and the corpsman said I probably had malaria.

"I can't have malaria," I told him, "I've only been here six days."

Then he saw my arm.

They took me to Charlie Med. Remember, this was in combat days, so they constantly had critical injuries coming in. They looked me over and told me they were going to have to do surgery. But they were out of anesthesia.

"We may have to cut your arm off," they told me.

I was very sick by this point, but I was firm. "You can't cut my arm off," I told them. "I paid thirteen dollars for that tattoo!"

They tied me face down to a table with large straps all over it and put a piece of hard rubber in my mouth to bite on. The Navy doctor leaned in close and said, "We're going to get started. Now, let's see how tough you are, Marine!" He kept saying it, trying to talk me through the pain.

I can't even describe how painful it was because they had to get rid of all the infection. Eventually, when everything that needed to be cut out was gone, the Doc asked me, "Would you like to see your arm bone before I close it up?"

"Sure," I mumbled. So, they held up a mirror, and I found myself looking at four inches of my arm bone. But now that they'd cut out the infection, they had to sew their way out, stitching the muscles back together again. That hour and a half surgery was one painful moment, to say the least!

I spent ten days in an air-conditioned tent in the Charlie Med equivalent of ICU, with them watching me carefully to see if I'd lose the arm. Thankfully, I didn't—that tattoo had been expensive!

In a weird way, I feel like God was protecting me even then. The patrol I would've gone on got shot up badly, and I was told that Singer, the other radio operator, got shot in the butt. At least he lived, but I never saw him again.

As I said, I spent ten days in the air-conditioned tent, then another seven in a regular hospital tent trying to heal up. After seventeen days in the hospital, they sent me back to my unit. When I got there, I found our unit was getting to take a break at China Beach, which was a rare opportunity. One of the Marines in the squad I would be joining asked to see my arm, and when I flexed my arm to show him, the wound burst open again! So back to Charlie Med I went for twenty more days.

In total, I spent thirty-seven days of my first forty-five days in Vietnam in a hospital bed. And, worse, they don't give Purple Hearts for being bitten by supply sergeants.

There were, however, side benefits to not ratting one out. I didn't tell a soul who had bitten me, and in thanks, he made sure my patrol and I had gear no one else could get. When you couldn't get jungle boots, I did! Also, you couldn't get doggy pouches—bags for your ammo magazines. We were supposed to have four, each of which would hold five magazines of twenty rounds because there was nowhere to get extras when you were out in the field in a firefight.

I also carried four fragmentation grenades, a white phosphorus, two smokes, and all the water you'd need for ten days. You also brought your food. I further carry a twenty-five pound PRC (the radio) and two batteries. All told, it was about a hundred pounds!

The first time I jumped off my helicopter into the elephant grass, I fell flat on my back! Elephant grass looks like natural grass—but it's six feet high. Everyone else hit the ground and took off running, but I was like a turtle on my back, trying to get back on my feet.

Eventually, one of the guys showed me how much stuff I could do without. For instance, you didn't need the whole case of sea rations, which was our food, so they showed me how to make sure I carried only the stuff I was sure to need.

As Recon, we were the ones without flak jackets or even helmets heading off into the jungle to get reconnaissance on enemy movements. Normally, we didn't do what regular grunts did, but one time they sent us out towards what was called Marble Mountain and handed us these E-Tools—a small shovel—and told us to dig in around this village. Apparently, they were expecting a big push from the North Vietnamese Regular Army—the NVA.

Those guys were excellent soldiers—well trained and very good at moving through the jungles. We were told to dig in and expect a big offensive, but the ground was so hard we could only get down about six inches. "Well," I said to my friends, "if they come, at least our kneecaps will be safe!"

Night came, and no one could see anything. It was totally pitch black. But we could hear something coming. (In those days, my hearing was pretty good; now the Marines pay for hearing aids.) This guy next to me opened fire with his M60 machine gun, and suddenly you could see everything in the flashes from the muzzle. It was an adrenaline rush!

Nobody had said "fire," however, so he stopped, but out in the darkness fifty or seventy yards out we could hear this screaming. It was horrible, and it just kept going and going.

A long night passed, and eventually morning came. There was no NVA attack, just a lot of lost sleep and anxious hours. In the growing light of day, we looked out to see what had been hit.

It was a pig! He'd shot up a pig, and it had screamed all night long. We were supposed to have taken the brunt of the NVA attack, but they'd heard that pig and had decided to hit a different place because they didn't know what it was either.

He had to pay for the pig, and that was irritating at the time, but it's entirely possible that pig saved our lives! It was just one of many moments where I now think God was preserving me in Vietnam.

I ended up doing sixteen long-range patrols from ten days to two weeks in length. I could feel God with me constantly.

Several of the guys in my patrol could feel it, too. If stuff started to hit the fan, they would say, "Get around Bess. He's got an aura around him—he can't be killed."

I was not living for the Lord at all, but His love and grace followed me through all my patrols in Vietnam. Over and over, things happened, but somehow, I, along with the rest of my patrol, remained safe.

Sometimes in our anger over life, we cannot hear the words of love very well from God or anyone else. I know for me it was hard and I was a little fearful of truly being loved. I was so angry in my grief that it was not just God that I responded badly to; many times it was people around me.

If you have ever been down that road of anger with all its condemnation, you know how hard it is to feel love or give it. Yet right there, our Lord loves us without any condemning. John 3:17 NIV says, *"For God did not send his Son into the world to condemn the world, but to save the world through him."*

I knew if I could be free of condemnation ever again I could be free from anger and that is what I found in Jesus the Christ, a brand-new nature! Wow!

"Therefore there is now no condemnation to those who are in Christ Jesus" (Romans 8:1 NIV).

"Therefore, if anyone is in Christ, he is a new creation; the old has gone, the new has come! All this is from God…" (2 Corinthians 5:17-18 NIV 1984).

CHAPTER 9:

SURROUNDED AND LEFT FOR DEAD

Because I was drop-certified and had jumped out of airplanes in the States, when they asked who wanted to do a jump in Vietnam, I volunteered. I wanted to get ten jumps in, at which point I'd get my gold wings.

Jumping was different in Vietnam, however. They flew in low, and you had to carry all the gear you'd need for a full patrol—ten to fourteen days' worth—so you had a lot of weight. However, the air was so moist, when we pulled our chutes, we just hung there! We seemingly couldn't come down, so we were just floating there. We thought we were targets for the enemy to shoot at.

I was coming in, finally, so I pulled the cord and dropped my rifle about six feet below me. You couldn't do a good landing with your rifle strapped to your leg because it was so stiff it would break your leg. So, you had to cut it away five or six feet before you hit the ground.

I landed just outside a village, and I looked back toward my rifle to see these kids picking it up. It was a very strange feeling; I'd heard all the horror stories about kids and entire villages being hostile. So, I had no idea what these kids were about to do. They could be about to kill me with my own rifle, and there was nothing I could do.

However, instead of killing me, this one little boy just held it out to me. I gave him a piece of gum, and he was pumped!

A few days later after our jump we went back on patrol, but like normal they dropped us off in a helicopter. We were deep inside NVA territory to recon the enemy strength. When doing recon, we avoided the trails; you couldn't get intelligence on a trail, because that's good and where the enemy would be. We went off the trails, moving through the jungle where they couldn't see you. Dressed in our greens and camouflage, our faces painted, you couldn't see us. But we could see the enemy, because they were on the trail.

We were taking a brief rest—we called it "harboring"—on the top of this hill, a heavily trafficked area we called Charlie Ridge. We had a new guy with us this time, and I told the lieutenant that I wanted to take him with me down over this edge to have him listen near the trail. McDowell, the guy with the M60 who'd shot the pig, was supposed to be on watch, but while we were gone, he fell asleep.

When he woke up, there were NVA soldiers *right there* nearly on top of him!

McDowell was lying on his back, and before the enemy soldiers could notice him and attack, he opened fire. He tore up the jungle with bullets, but he didn't kill them. They ran down the trail, but others in our group popped up and shot them. Because we were on recon, we had to take everything—we needed every piece of intelligence we could get.

No sooner did we finish searching them for info, then we looked up to see the hill above us appeared to have ants crawling on it. Except they weren't ants, they were enemy soldiers! Literally hundreds of them were pouring off the top of the hill because they had heard the gunshots.

We started moving through the jungle as quickly as we could, but they were very close. Suddenly everything broke loose—bullets flying everywhere, Claymore mines and grenades exploding, everything! We went as far as we could, but the sheer volume of fire coming at us made it impossible to get away. We were closed in by the enemy and couldn't get away.

The enemy soldiers were getting closer; they would soon get close enough to surround and kill us all. We were on the move firing our rifles, M-79 grenade launcher, M60 machine gun, and at times throwing grenades.

I turned to the lieutenant and said, "If we're going to go, let's go out in glory!"

He nodded. "Do it," he said.

I got on the radio and called for fire support from the Army. We were Marines, but the Army had bigger howitzers that could shoot further. They had 175mm Howitzers. Their call sign was "Fudge Cake Alfa," and ours was "Blue Spruce Romeo." So I called, "Fudge Cake Alfa, this is Blue Spruce Romeo, fire on grind square," which was our location.

"Fire for effect," I yelled into the radio, after giving the artillery our exact location that was right on top of our own position. This is what I meant by going out in glory; the enemy was so close, the artillery might blow us up, but it would kill the enemy at the same time. Above all, we did not want to let them capture us, because they would torture recon Marines for days trying to learn any intelligence we might know. It was better to be blown up by our own artillery than that!

I'd called the artillery fire request in to the Army, because their bigger guns could shoot further. Far away, I could hear the boom of all six 175mm howitzers firing. When the shells come in, they *scream*. They're very loud as they shriek in, and as they came in we all hit the ground as low as we could get.

Explosions shattered the jungle, louder than can be believed. Shrapnel buzz sawed through the trees like a million angry bees, the explosives and the flying metal mowing down trees and people alike. The six blasts shredded the jungle all around us.

In the aftermath of the explosions, it was silent. It was eerie. In that dead silence, I suddenly realized I was *alive!* Not only that, I checked myself for injuries and found that I was all in one piece. Slowly I stood up, and I saw our patrol leader also stand to his feet. One by one, the other five guys all stood up.

Despite how close the artillery explosions were, we all emerged alive with no injuries. The Marines would be paying for hearing aids for us all sometime in the future.

"Typical Army," I said. "They *missed!*"

We all began laughing in the nervous way the people do when they have just looked right in the face of death but lived to tell about it. However, the Army didn't completely miss—out across the area where dozens or hundreds of enemy soldiers had just been, nothing moved. All the machine-gun fire and grenades had stopped, and we were momentarily alone in the shattered jungle.

By this point, they had dispatched an aerial observer: an airplane above us looking down from above at our situation. As the radio operator, I got in contact with him. He told me to pop smoke, so we set off a smoke grenade.

We knew the enemy was listening in on the radio, so he said, "I got two," which meant to set off a red smoke grenade. So, we popped off a red, and he told me, "I got you."

Now that he knew our position, he could see where we were in relation to the other North Vietnamese soldiers. "It looks like ants down there," he told me.

I said, "They sure aren't ants!" The AO (aerial observer) called in two F4 Phantoms as air support, and as the first one flew over he was shot down by the enemy. The AO called the second one off and began to give us instructions on how to get to an LZ (Landing Zone) so we could get extracted out.

Because of this jungle canopy, the helicopter could not land just anywhere; they had to give us directions to a place where the helicopter could get close enough for us to get on. He gave me instructions, and for the next hour and a half we ran for all we were worth toward a landing zone on the side of the hill. But the aerial observer couldn't see the terrain we had to cover; he could just tell us the direction. We had to move through thick jungle; but it wasn't just trees, it was also ridges and hills and ravines and streams.

Each of us was carrying full packs, and running through the jungle is difficult work in any circumstance. After an hour and a half, we were all completely exhausted. We could barely function, and we were ready to collapse. However, after what seemed an eternity we reached the landing zone.

The "LZ" was on the side of the hill, and finally we could hear the helicopters coming! The gunships flew very low over the jungle and began circling. Door gunners were leaning out and shooting all around, trying to keep the enemy down. We were in the middle of a circling group of gunships, and then our helicopter, an H46, began to descend. However, he could not land because we were on the side of a hill, so he was hovering.

One by one, we began to board the helicopter. We had to jump. I was to be the last one on, because I was the primary radio operator. Everyone got on board, and then it was my turn.

I had to get the timing right, and when the pilot dipped, I was to jump. The helicopter crew would pull me in. I threw my rifle up ahead of me, but just as I jumped, the helicopter came up and hit me in the chest! The crew tried to grab me, but they missed.

Instead of making it into the helicopter and safety, I went tumbling down the hill, over a hundred pounds on my back making my roll hard to stop. And my rifle was on the helicopter!

I reached out and tried to grab grass or trees to stop my tumble, but nothing seemed to work. Finally, I grabbed onto something and stopped my downhill plunge.

Suddenly I could hear NVA soldiers yelling, and I managed to get my feet under me and to the top of that hill in record time! But no sooner did I get back to where I was, then I realized I could no longer hear the helicopters.

The only sounds were the Vietnamese soldiers coming. I was alone; they'd left me.

I still had my radio, so I immediately got on the radio and asked where everybody had gone. "I'm right here!" I yelled. "Come back!"

The enemy soldiers were so close I could hear them talking now. I didn't have my rifle, but somehow, I still had two fragmentation grenades. I figured I would throw one and hold on to the other. I would throw the first, and then I would hold on to the second and run towards enemy soldiers, trying to take a few of them with me. I wasn't going to let them take me!

I was straightening the pins on my grenades to get ready when I heard the most amazing sound in the world: the helicopters were coming back! With NVA soldiers closing in all around me, the gunships came back just over the top of the trees and the gunners fired into the jungle. The H46 descended to pick me up. I somehow managed to get aboard, thankful just to be alive.

But it wasn't over yet.

The aerial observer was still circling around up there, and he had called in the big boys—F-4 fighter planes. Remember, the NVA had shot one down, blowing them right out of the sky. The aerial observer thought he had seen a parachute, so they directed our helicopters to where the plane had gone down.

We got there, but it was a disaster. The jet had hit the jungle and exploded, scattering burning bits of wreckage all over the jungle. I got out of the helicopter with some of the rest of our squad, but they were all standing around. I went to see what they were looking at.

If the pilots had tried to eject, they did so too late—there were pieces of them all over. We all just stood there, completely shell shocked. No one wanted to touch anything, but Marines don't like to leave anyone behind. I grabbed my poncho and started picking up anything I could. It was unbelievable, and I tried not to think about what I was touching as I wrapped up my poncho around what used to be United States Marine Pilots. It's hard to explain what you feel in those moments. I was filled with sadness that they had died and honored that I had the privilege of bringing them home.

When we finally landed back at Charlie Med again, I handed the Corpsman my poncho. There wasn't enough left to need a gurney.

They determined that the remains we'd recovered were just from one man. The aerial observer perhaps had seen a parachute from the other pilot. And if he was out there, we would not leave him to the North Vietnamese army.

The next day, we loaded up three helicopters full of Marines. We were going after the second pilot. The problem was that the NVA knew we didn't leave people behind, so they would most likely be ready for us.

I was in the first helicopter with the lieutenant, our patrol leader, but he sent me to take over the second helicopter and asked me to send the secondary radio operator up to the first helicopter. He was preparing me to eventually be a patrol leader, which I would later become, but on this day not being with the lieutenant would save my life.

The helicopters flew low over the jungle, and as we got deeper into enemy territory, as the first helicopter descended something hit it. It was on fire rolling down a hill! The other two helicopters veered off, and they took us out of there. They flew us to An Hoa and put us at the end of the runway and told us to just sit there.

We were all Recon Marines, but we were sitting there sobbing for what we had seen at what appeared as the loss of our friends. However, by the end of that day, everyone on that helicopter that went down was rescued and alive. We were pumped!

Remember, during all this I was not living for the Lord. The few times I had the opportunity, I would get drunk and start quoting the Gospel of John to anyone who would listen. In fact, I became notorious for it! I couldn't remember a word of what I said, but everyone told me that when I got drunk I always began to preach to them.

Throughout all those journeys into the jungles of Vietnam, even though I was angry with God for letting Larry die, He was with me. As I said, it felt like God was right on my shoulder, and He was looking out for me. Somehow, God preserved me through all my patrols, being chased by what turned out to be somewhere near *a thousand* Vietnamese soldiers, and even being left for dead. If I had been on that first helicopter on that would-be rescue mission, I would've been shot down. God switched me to the second chopper and preserved my life.

I didn't know why. But I could feel Him. I often told Him to get off my back, but He never did. In fact, the other guys in my squad could feel something—that God was with me even though I was not being faithful to Him then.

The Bible tells us, "*This is a trustworthy saying: If we die with him, we will also live with him. If we endure hardship, we will reign with him. If we deny him, he will deny us. If we are unfaithful, he remains faithful, for he cannot deny who he is*" (2 Timothy 2:11-13 NLT).

God isn't faithful because of the good things we do for Him; He is faithful because that's who He is. We cannot earn His grace and mercy to us, and even when we proved to be unfaithful servants who experience doubts and fears and uncertainty—even when we are angry with Him!—He remains faithful.

Even though I was very angry with God for letting Larry die, I without a doubt experienced His faithfulness in the jungles of Vietnam; and I am alive today to tell you that no matter what, God is faithful. He surrounds us with His faithfulness.

CHAPTER 10:

RETURN OF AN ANGRY MAN

I eventually went on sixteen long-range patrols and did become a patrol leader. However, I was asked to go to recon headquarters service, and one of my assignments was to go out to an observation post on the top of the jungle hill where I would man a radio relay for a few days. I was protected by a platoon of Marine grunts. It was just to be for a few days, so they told me that I would only need to take my rifle.

The only problem was…they forgot about me! A few days assignment turned into *fifty* days, and I had nothing with me but the clothes I was wearing—not even a toothbrush. I did have food and water, so there's that.

When I got off the helicopter after those fifty long days in the jungle, I was a sight to see. I hadn't shaved during that time, and I had been in the moist jungle of Vietnam. My Marine clothing was in bad shape, and I smelled horrible!

I remember walking beneath the wooden tori—a type of wooden Japanese arch—of the landing zone as I came back. When you are headed out on patrol, you would walk under a sign that said, "Under this tori passes the greatest fighting man in the world." Coming back, it said, "Reenlist! Free helicopter rides."

I always enjoyed seeing it!

A recon colonel came up to me and put his arm around my shoulders, disregarding my stink and generally less than shipshape grooming. As he walked with me, he said to me, "Son, you are what make the Marines proud. I'll bet you're hungry. How about a steak?"

"Yes sir!" I answered. I remember then asking, "We have steak in Vietnam?"

They did. I ate two!

When I got back to my hooch, everyone wondered where I'd been. I told them they forgot about me, and the guys were good enough to help me scrub the green jungle rot off my back. My clothes literally had fallen apart around me, and I had green blotches on my skin and jungle rot on my ankles where the skin was just gooey.

I had a lot of other assignments in my time in Vietnam; I was there a total of thirteen months. They wanted me to re-up, of course, and encouraged me to take a test to become an officer, so I took a test and passed it. I wanted to be a pilot, and I passed that test, too! I was going to get a $10,000 bonus to sign up, and they were going to send me to officer's school and flight school. I was ready to do it. However, for some reason I simply couldn't sign the paperwork.

They told me not to worry about it and that I had three months to think it over. Another friend of mine, Carl Snyder, took the test as well. We got out about the same time, but he went back after about fifty days and signed his paperwork. He then started training to become an officer and a pilot. But I couldn't—even though I thought that's what I wanted to do, I just couldn't sign that paperwork.

I didn't become an officer or a helicopter pilot, but Carl did. To my great sadness, He was killed in the evacuation of Vietnam in 1975.

I headed back to California where my parents picked me up and gave me a place to live. The jungle rot quickly faded in the dry desert conditions of Southern California, but the clinging after effects of the fighting and killing that I had seen clung to me. The physical signs of my tour lasted a short time, but I seemed to have developed an anger problem that would last for several years.

I now understood what my father had felt like after returning from World War II. And he understood me, too, probably far more than anyone else. In fact, he and I got along better after I got back from Vietnam than any other time in my life.

Because I had seen so much combat, I was tough. I had a foul mouth, and it shocked my mom. But my dad told her that it was okay; he understood what it's like to be in that kind of combat. You cannot come back normal, and you're just not the same. I had gone through a transition much like he had, and he understood where I was coming from. We could talk honestly about "stuff," because we now had common ground.

After I had been home for a little while, the CIA showed up. My dad was there and heard what they had to say. "We want you to work for us," they told me. "We want to give you a job—the same thing you did in Vietnam, except you'll do it in Africa, and we will pay you and train you. We'll pay you a lot more than you made in the Marines; we will start you at $50,000 a year."

In 1969, that was a whole lot of money! After telling me their offer, they gave me one week to think it over. My dad and I began to talk about it, and he immediately told me that he didn't want me to do it. I think he probably understood what would be involved in working for the CIA.

In the end, my dad talked me out of going. I think I would've gone without him there—the lure of $50,000 a year, the super training, and the appeal of being in intelligence work was strong. However, my dad kept a level head; I believe God was using him to speak wisdom into my life.

Instead of joining the CIA and fighting in Africa, I did the next most logical thing: I bought a motorcycle, a Triumph.

It was very difficult to adjust to life back in the States. Protesters against the Vietnam War, many of them hippies, seemed to be insulting the very people who were dying over there—my friends. It seemed like the whole country was against us, totally unappreciative of the lives being lost over there fighting communism. My brother Marines were fighting and dying to keep the oppressive shadow of communism from spreading, and at home what I thought were privileged idiots were taking out their anger on the very people fighting to protect their way of life.

A friend of mine, Frank, came out of the Marines with me. He and I bought motorcycles together and rode around the country having what we thought was fun. The only problem was that I was incredibly angry and broken inside, and "fun" involved drinking, topless joints, and some violence. I carried weapons around with me—a .357 Python revolver, a knife, and even a hatchet.

We now understand the problems of coming back far better than they did then, and I likely would have been diagnosed with PTSD today. I reacted to everything, drank a lot, and spent my time doing things like playing pool and getting into trouble.

I remember being in my family's yard and doing some yard work one time when this platinum blond-haired hippie walked past their house and started harassing me. I was on my hands and knees cutting grass with these giant scissors, and this guy kept shooting off his mouth.

"Do yourself a favor," I told him, "and just move on." But he didn't stop. He could see by my high and tight haircut and demeanor that I definitely looked military and put together. He pressed on and asked if I had been in Vietnam. I responded by telling him I just got back. "Do yourself a favor," I said, "move on."

He ended up calling me a murderer, and in the blink of an eye I had knocked him to the ground and put these giant scissors to his throat. "Don't even think of moving," (I actually used more colorful language than that, but you get the idea.)

So, I took those giant scissors and began to cut off his beautiful platinum blond hair! "You do not ever want to see me again," I told him, and I know I scared the daylights out of him!

I never saw him again, and miraculously I didn't get charged with assault, but it just illustrates the seething anger just under the surface in my life. At this point in time, I was a nice former Marine with an anger problem.

Another time, I was playing pool with some guys when another hippie came in. I was sitting at the bar minding my own business when this guy started running his mouth. I told him to leave me alone, but again he just wouldn't leave well enough alone. I'm grateful I didn't pull the .357 magnum revolver in my boot or the knife I kept in my pocket. (Remember, in addition to being a Marine, I had also been a Boy Scout —I was always prepared!)

But the guy kept pushing, and so I decided to leave, but my anger was exploding. I walked out the back door of the bar, intending to leave, but this guy stood at the back door, continuing to insult me as a former Marine. That did it! I lifted the seat of my motorcycle, grabbed the hatchet I kept under there, and was going to come back and plant it right in his head. I was walking back towards him…when suddenly the door to the bar just slammed shut right in my face!

This guy had worked me up into a murderous rage, and I had every intention of burying the hatchet—right in his forehead! But instead, my hatchet got buried in the back door of this bar! It was extremely hard to get it out! And, what's more, there was no one there to shut the door; it simply slammed shut on its own, right into the path of my hatchet.

By the time I got it out, the guy was gone. I got on my motorcycle, and I realized I probably needed to leave town for a while. Frank and I didn't just leave Los Angeles, though; over the next month we went all the way to the state line of New York. It was a beautiful, scenic ride, and in those days very few people were riding motorcycles. With Triumph's motorcycles, you had to stop every five hundred miles and tighten everything down…or it would fall off the next day.

I remember getting out east and calling my parents. "The whole country sucks," I told them. "I don't want to live here anymore."

Eventually, I decided to head back. I stopped in Cheyenne, Wyoming, and the people there were very nice to me—so nice I almost decided to stay. However, I went home and got my job back with Douglas Aircraft. I didn't really like it, and so after a few months I got into the roofing business with my friend Jack, who had gone into the Navy.

But I kept getting into trouble. It was New Year's Eve, 1969, and Rick—who had gone into the Army and went to Vietnam—and Al, another former Marine—who never made it to Vietnam but got as far as Okinawa—and I were out partying. After all, it was New Year's Eve. We had been playing pool, drinking a lot, and got a bottle of vodka for the road. We were driving down a dirt road somewhere in the San Fernando Valley when Al said he had to use the head (bathroom). I was driving my truck, so I pulled over and let Al do his business.

While he was busy doing his business, he saw a street sign. He shook it a bit and then pulled it out of the ground, the cement still attached and everything! Al was a skinny guy, but he was strong. We thought that was cool, so we threw it in the back of a truck and then decided to drive around, seeing what other kinds of signs we could find. Al pulled them up and threw them in the back of the truck. This was great fun—we were obviously totally smashed!

"You know," Al said, "your mom and dad need new trash cans." So, we drove by some nice neighborhood and grabbed a few brand-new looking trash cans. We dumped the trash out and threw them in the back of my truck.

It was now 2:00 a.m. in the morning, and we had a pickup full of city signs and stolen trash cans. So, what do we decide to do? "Let's go get something to eat!"

I was driving too fast and blasting through the corner, running a light, when suddenly there was a policeman! I pulled into a café, and guess who pulled in behind us?

I turned to Rick and Al and said, "Don't tell him we have those street signs underneath the trash cans."

So, the policeman comes to the window, and I roll it down. What's the very first thing out of my mouth? "We don't have street signs underneath the trash cans."

"I need you to step out of the car, sir," he said to me. Meanwhile, two more LAPD patrol cars pull up. We were in trouble!

We were so drunk, we thought all this was hysterical. We were laughing, and the first policeman saw our attitude and suddenly slammed me up against my truck, turned me around, and started cursing me out. "You think this is funny?" he asked, cursing at me liberally.

Both Al and Rick were saying my name over and over, trying to keep me calm. They knew that if I wanted to, I could probably kill this cop in a fit of rage.

Abruptly, he let me go and went back to talk to his fellow cops. They started laughing, including the guy who had just slammed me up against my truck. I was fit to be tied! I walked over to him and slammed him against his car and then said the same words to him that he had just said to me!

They did not like that. Suddenly, I was in handcuffs, and they picked me up and threw me into the back of a squad car. Now I was *really* angry! I was going to try to do harm to this policeman. I started working the handcuffs around underneath me with the intent to strangle him. But then I thought, they handcuffed me with my hands behind me, and I now had them in front. I didn't want them to see me, so I put them behind me again.

When the policeman got into his car, I tried to bring my hands into the front of me again, but something unbelievable took place—a hand came out of the backseat and held the chain of the handcuffs so that I could not get them underneath me. It wouldn't let me go!

People talk about guardian angels, and I know that I gave mine such a workout! I could literally feel the fingers of the hand holding the chain, preventing me from bringing those cuffs in front of me.

But God wasn't done preserving me. I kept receiving His favor, even though I didn't deserve it.

I look back on those days in wonder how I had made it through without killing myself or anyone else. I could never have guessed what God was going to do with me at that point. Never!

You may be in a dark place right now. You may wonder where your life is going and despair of ever seeing anything change. Maybe you're angry or depressed or grieving, and you don't see light at the end of your tunnel.

I couldn't see a future for myself through this haze of alcohol, violence, and anger that threatened to consume my life.

But Jesus did.

Some people really struggle with why God does not prevent bad things from happening or keep us from going through rough times. The thing is, the Bible does not promise us we will never go through difficult times. In fact, just the opposite—Jesus knew that in this world we would have trouble.

In John 16:33 He says, *"I have told you all this so that you may have peace in me. Here on earth you will have many trials and sorrows. But take heart, because I have overcome the world"* (NLT).

We can have peace, even in the middle of trouble, because Jesus has gone before us. He paved the way, so even when we don't know and can't even guess what the future holds, we can stand on the promise that ultimately, He has won the war.

You have no idea what can happen in your life when your whole goal, your whole desire, is to know God. We think the things that have hurt us, that we've done or that have happened to us, disqualify us from His plans, but this isn't true.

When we're in it not to get something, even to be saved, but to know Him, you have no idea what will take place. I don't mean that you're not going to have hard times; we're all going to experience hard spots in life. I mean that in His presence, chasing after knowing Him, hard times pale in comparison to the goodness He has planned for your life.

When I returned from Vietnam, I was a long way from God, and in fact I had turned my back on Him in anger for letting my friend die. But what I didn't know was that there is no back you can turn to Him when He is *in you.*

David, the psalmist, writes, *"Where can I go from Your Spirit? Or where can I flee from Your presence? If I ascend into heaven, You are there; if I make my bed in hell, behold, You are there.... Even there Your hand shall lead me, and Your right hand shall hold me"* (Psalm 139:7-8,10).

I thought I could turn my back on God, but I didn't know there was nothing that could separate me from His love. God doesn't judge us by our behavior; He judges us by what Christ Jesus did for us. It's Christ, period.

CHAPTER 11:

MEETING KAREN

Instead of hurting anyone, I went to jail. I used my phone call to call my mom (it was now 3:00 in the morning). When I told her I was in jail, she asked, "What do you want me to do about it?" and hung up!

I turned to the policeman, the one I'd been so angry with, and asked, "Can I make another call?"

"Nope," he answered, "it's just like the movies—you only get one."

So, I stayed in jail that night, but in the morning Rick and Al bailed me out. My mom did end up hiring a lawyer, and it was a good thing because I almost got myself in trouble again.

My lawyer told me that the judge was a retired First Sergeant from the Marine Corps, and I thought that being in front of a former combat Marine would help. My lawyer told the judge about all my combat experience, I think hoping it would help. Then the prosecuting attorney laid out the charges—and there were a lot of them, because I was getting charged for everything even though I was only driving—and then I awaited the judge's decision. He said, "I'm a retired First Sergeant of the United States Marine Corps, and I expect more out of Marines than any other people on the planet; therefore I sentence you to the maximum sentence I can give—a six hundred and fifty dollar fine and six months in jail."

My rage exploded. I said, "You come down from behind that desk and take off that black robe, and we'll see who's going to jail!"

But my lawyer put his hand over my mouth and then said to me, "Shut up!" He jumped up, said something to the judge, and came back to me and said again, "Shut up!" And then he took me out of the courtroom.

We then went into another courtroom and stood at the back, and my lawyer said to me, "Don't you say a word." In a very short time the judge that was in that courtroom motioned for my lawyer to come forward.

My lawyer went up to the judge and whispered something. The judge looked at me and said, "Call him up."

As my lawyer walked me up, he again told me to not say a thing. Then something happened that really surprised me. The judge said that he found me guilty as charged, but for each thing he found me guilty of, he said it was suspended. Finally, they changed the fine from six hundred and fifty dollars to a hundred and fifty. And, since I'd already paid the bailer six fifty, I got five hundred dollars back.

As we were walking out, I was still completely stunned. I asked the lawyer, "How did you do that?"

"That's what your mother paid me for," he told me. Then he looked at me very meaningfully and said, "Young man, you need to think about doing something else with your life."

I said, "Well, I tell you one thing."

"What's that?"

"I'll never be here again! Whatever I may do, I'm never going to do something this stupid ever again."

Thanks to God's grace, I never did.

Aside from getting drunk, getting in trouble, anger issues, and carrying weapons about on my person I was all too likely to use, things were going well. I was making money as a roofer. It was hard work, but I've never been afraid of honest, hard work. I was even dating a lot, though mostly it involved going out to dinner just to listen to the young woman I was with talk about life.

In fact, I was going out and talking with a rather wide variety of girls at the same time and had *four* young women I was dating! I was not, however, thinking of getting married to any of them. I really liked my freedom.

Yet I felt this aching emptiness, this vacancy in my life. I was not serving God at all. It was in this state, less than two weeks after getting off with the one hundred and fifty dollar fine that I found myself in the backseat of the race car that Rick owned and feeling introspective. I remember that I had a good luck fifty-cent piece my grandfather gave me in my hand, just feeling it. I'd carried it all through Vietnam for good luck.

Now as I looked at it, the words "In God We Trust" caught my eye. I hadn't talked to God in months, except to tell Him to get off my back in Vietnam, but the emptiness in my life was overwhelming me.

So, I prayed to the God on our money: "I want to make a deal." Then I thought, I can't make a deal with God because if He is God, He needs nothing, and therefore I have nothing to offer. But then this thought came to me. "If You're God, You know everything about me already, so You know I'm not lying. If You'll do something with my life…I'd even be willing to get married." I knew that He knew that I did not want to ever get married. So the sacrifice was offered.

I am not exaggerating when I say that perhaps ten minutes later, I walked into the People's Tree, a nightclub near Malibu Canyon and saw the woman who would change my life forever! There were hundreds of people in this club, but it was like a light was on her.

I knew nothing about her, but I was instantly in love.

I turned to Rick and said, "Another cowboy just fell out of the saddle." He didn't understand, so I said, "You see that blonde over there? I'm in love with her!"

"You can't be in love with her," he told me frankly. "You don't even know her!"

I'd never felt anything like this before; it was the most amazing feeling, radiating out from my chest. I knew something was different with her.

I asked her to dance, and we danced all night long. But I was so overwhelmed; I didn't even get her number. And then she left!

I knew her name was Karen.

The next day, I couldn't get her out of my heart. It was a Sunday, and so I went back to the club that night—no Karen. I went back Monday night, and again she wasn't there. Tuesday, Wednesday, Thursday, and still she wasn't there. Many of the young women in the club would ask me to dance, but I just couldn't—I just sat there. I didn't want Karen to walk in and see me dancing with another girl.

On Friday, I got off work and decided to go to the nightclub at 5:30 in the afternoon for some reason. I usually went there about 9:30 and stayed until midnight. When I walked into that nightclub that afternoon, to my joy and surprise, there was Karen! She was the only one there.

I immediately went over to her and was thrilled that she remembered me. We sat down together and shared some drinks, and I thought it was going well. I was hoping that she would like to go out on a date together, so I asked her out.

I wasn't expecting her response: "You don't want to go out with me."

I didn't understand; it seemed to be going so well. "I'm sorry, was I rude?" I asked.

"No," she told me, shaking her head.

"Then why should I not want to go out with you?"

She hesitated. "I've been married before," she told me.

"Married before? How old are you?" I asked, and she said she was twenty-one. I was just twenty-two. "And you've already been married and divorced?" I asked.

"Yeah," she replied. (What she didn't tell me then was that she also had two children, but it wouldn't have changed anything.)

I said to her, "I am not talking about marriage. I am asking if you will go out with me tonight." She saw I wasn't going away, so she eventually said yes. We made plans for me to pick her up at her place.

We went our separate ways—me to my home to get ready, her to hers. I wanted to take her somewhere special, and I immediately thought of the Whisky A Go Go in Hollywood. Except you couldn't get in there, not on a Friday night.

But I knew I could get us in.

I picked Karen up in my truck, and we headed to the club. The line stretched three or four blocks, but I ignored the line. I walked right up to the front, and the bouncer looked at me. "Gus," he said, and *boom* we were in!

I was really enjoying the moment of walking right into the nightclub with Karen.

Movie stars and television celebrities were there, together with musicians and other famous people. *The Mod Squad* was big back then as a television series, and they were seated at a table. I took us by and introduced Karen to them.

We sat down with them, and then a problem took place. They had all been there for some time and had been drinking large amounts. The next thing I knew, "Linc" (Clarence Williams) passed out on the floor.

"Want to get out of here?" I asked, leading Karen away from the scene.

"Yeah."

So, we went from the hippest nightclub in LA…to Denny's! It was probably the only thing open that late for dinner. I'd never taken a date to Denny's, but then I'd never dated Karen before.

I wouldn't ever need to date anyone else again.

Karen had her own backstory, of course. She now freely shares what a mess her life was in at that point. She was divorced, as she'd mentioned, and she also had two children from her marriage. Her mom was looking after them the night we met, but because of back trouble, her mom couldn't help as much as she'd like with the kids. Karen faced the challenge of trying to work and find good, caring people to help with them.

Karen was going through a dark depression at this point in her life crushed under a spirit of despair. It was so bad that she was missing a lot of work, and she was struggling to just get up out of bed and function. The weight of it all was crushing the life out of her, and while she didn't know Jesus at that point, she talked to God all the time and was begging Him for His help.

In fact, when we met, she was losing her job because she'd missed so much work. She didn't know what to do with the kids and didn't know what she was going to do with her *life*. Karen's life was just spiraling downward. She would let her ex-husband come and take the kids because she didn't know how she'd support them. Moving back home seemed like the likely outcome.

She felt like a total, complete failure.

The night we danced, a friend had invited her to go out and get around people to try to cheer her up, but she hadn't even wanted to go. She walked into the People's Tree nightclub that next Friday to just get a drink and was not expecting to see or talk to anyone, least of all me, the guy she didn't know had been looking for her night after night. No one else was at the club when she got there, and that suited her just fine.

Then I showed up.

She later shared with me that she was so depressed, while she recognized me, she couldn't even really respond. It was out of that deep depression and sense of complete failure that she told me I didn't want to go out with her. She was so low, she really didn't think anyone would *want* to be with her—or that she'd be good for anyone to date.

You may feel you're at the lowest point of your life right now, as Karen did. You may feel buried under depression and crushed under a sense of disappointment and failure. Things may look very black to you.

Or, like me, you may simply feel an emptiness in your life. Maybe it's like there's a hole in your heart, a place where you know something is *supposed to be* but instead feels like just an empty, aching chasm.

I hope that you're able to read about the dark, lonely places we have been and see that you are not alone. Karen and I have been to some very black places in our lives.

What may surprise you is that Jesus the Christ understands those times as well.

The Word of God tells us that we have a Savior who understands what it's like to be in our shoes. He can identify with what it's like to be a human being, with all the disappointments, pains, and loneliness that is part of the human condition.

You are not alone. No matter what you're going through, there is One who understands and who will never leave you or forsake you.

Karen and I didn't understand the depths of His love when we first met. She believed in God but didn't know Him as Jesus yet, and I had spent my entire time in Vietnam and afterward pushing Him away.

Neither of us were experiencing the fullness of His love. But He still loved us even when we did not know it.

We weren't feeling Jesus' presence, but we were both aching for a change.

If you are, too, I will not insult you by saying there is one magic prayer or one experience you lack that will fix all your problems. However, I will tell you that there is one *Person* out there, and it isn't that He is dangling the solutions to your problems like a carrot to lure you in...

He *is* the solution. It is all about *knowing* Him.

As I said at the beginning of this book, if there is a God, can there be anything greater than knowing Him? Is there any greater gift that He could give you than Himself?

No matter what you're going through, how dark it is, or how hopeless you are, know this: it's not about a solution or action you need to do.

There's a Person I want you to meet.

Karen and I met Him. He changed everything.

It didn't happen overnight, but as surely as the tide coming in His grace overwhelmed us and began remaking our lives. He didn't impose Himself, but as we welcomed Him, receiving His grace, something new began in us. They weren't silver bullets for our circumstances; they were changes *within us*. "*Therefore, if anyone is in Christ, he is a new creation; the old has gone, the new has come! All this is from God...*" (2 Corinthians 5:17-18 NIV 1984).

This happened because when we get to know Him, we start to become like Him. Want to know Him? I'd love to introduce you!

His name is Jesus the Christ!

CHAPTER 12:

BACK TO CHURCH

God was about to get ahold of my life, I just didn't know it yet.

It was a Sunday morning, I was twenty-one years old, and I was heading home after being out all night partying. I had been out of the Marine Corps for just over three months. I was riding my Triumph down Roscoe Boulevard, wearing my blue jeans and white t-shirt with the cut off sleeves, with my .357 magnum in my boot, a four-inch switchblade in my left pocket, a hatchet under my motorcycle seat, and a cigarette hanging from my lips. Suddenly, I saw a church as I rode by it. For some reason, I made a U-turn and parked my bike in front of the church.

Understand, I still believed that you couldn't go to church unless you were invited, so I don't know why I decided to pull into this church, but I did just as people were going in. They were all dressed nicely in suits and dresses, and I had no idea why I was going in, dressed the way I was.

But I did. I slipped into the back of the church, and something incredibly surprising was waiting for me. Guess who was preaching?

Allan Billington! This wasn't the same Baptist church building that he was at before. The church had moved to this new location while I was in the Marine Corps. What is so amazing is that I had heard they had moved but did not know where. I just *happened* to pull into the church's new location, and he was preaching that day. As I look back, this was definitely God at work in my life.

There were perhaps one hundred and fifty people in this little white church building, and as I sat in the back, I watched them respond to Allan's preaching. They would nod their heads and quietly say, "Uh-huh, amen," occasionally to something he said.

What in the world was that? It was strange, but I eventually figured that maybe he was nervous and they were trying to encourage him. I'm an encourager by nature, so I decided that if he said anything I understood I was going to encourage him too.

Finally, he said something I understood. So, I pointed at him and loudly said, "Uh-huh! Amen!"

When I said that, he stopped preaching. He took a couple of steps back, and when he saw me, he got a big grin on his face and said, "Yeah!"

Well, he resumed preaching, and I thought if he says anything again that I understand and agree with, I will do it again and so I did—but I didn't know it was the end of the service. The woman sitting right in front of me turned and said, "Why don't you get out of here?"

This woman ticked me off. I was about to respond to her attitude physically and verbally, but I didn't. I decided to do something else that would really annoy her—return the next week! I decided that wherever she was, I was going to sit right behind her!

Well, ironically, while I was there to irritate this woman (and it appeared at the time that I was successful), God was using this quirk of my personality to get me into church. There I heard Allan Billington preach the living breath of God, which in turn began making an impact on my life in ways I couldn't even fathom at the time.

(God has a terrific sense of humor.) Not only was being there to irritate this woman getting me into church, God was setting something up for years down the road. As a twenty-eight-year-old young man finishing Bible college, this woman's husband would ask me to talk to their son. Believe it or not, I worked for her husband by this point while I went to college! Their son, Mike, was in the eleventh grade, and they said he was rebellious, with long hair and not a clue about what he wanted to do with his life. However, somehow, he respected me.

So, I called his son Mike and set up a time to meet. We met in his 1962 Chevrolet truck for about two and a half hours. On that day, Mike committed his life and future to Jesus the Christ and never looked back. To this day, he is a great man of God!

There is no one like the Lord! At the time I walked into that church at age twenty-one and met Mike's mother, neither of us could have had any idea of what God would do through our unlikely meeting in the future. And, typical of the Lord, we would all be blessed.

Three months after I walked into that church, I would meet Karen, the beautiful woman God would choose for me to love, protect, and bless.

We had just taken a long motorcycle ride over what's called the Grapevine—a mountain pass out of Southern California that divided the Los Angeles basin from the fertile fields of San Joaquin Valley. We headed back to her apartment where we sat and talked. We met at the People's Tree Nightclub on the 16th of January, and this was now the 16th of February.

"You know, I can't imagine living the rest of my life without you," I told her.

To her ears, I was saying I wanted to get married! She immediately called her girlfriend and told her that we were getting married! I then told Karen that I knew a pastor who I thought would marry us. Her response to me was, *You know a pastor?"*

So, I called Allan and told him that I was going to get married. I asked him if he did weddings, and he said he did and asked us to come over to his office. So, we headed over to talk to Allan. We told him we wanted to get married on May 16th. That would be just one hundred and twenty days after we met!

At the meeting, Allan asked Karen, "Do you know the Lord?"

"I believe in Jesus," she answered. "I always have."

"No," Allan replied in his typical fashion, "do you *know* Him?" He picked up his Bible, and he began reading some Scriptures. You'll remember that I was unable to understand the tract with the Gospel of John before my experience with the Lord. Well, much like that, when she'd heard other Scriptures read or talked about in her past, Karen simply couldn't understand them.

But when Allan began reading, Karen told me later that it was like a bulb flashed in her mind and heart; she suddenly understood what the Scriptures were saying!

But as they talked, I started getting more and more angry. In fact, I got up and walked out. I was still struggling with emotions that were extremely raw because Jesus did not keep my friend Larry alive. I did not want Karen to become a "Christian woman." At that time in my life, the Christian women I had met were very critical and (in my opinion at the time) downright ugly, inside and out. So, I did not want her to become one of those.

Allan led Karen to the Lord while I was out of the room. She was hungry for God, and the way Allan stated it—that it was about actually *knowing* God, not just knowing *about* Him—really got ahold of her. On that day, Karen received God's gift of grace in Jesus Christ, and she became a new creation.

However, while that is all true, I was becoming more irritated. We planned the wedding, and Karen was very excited but I was truly struggling. In fact, on the day of the wedding, we had about 120 people there in the chapel. I was standing in front with Allan Billington, my best man, and two other groomsmen. The music started, and the brides-maids were making their way to the front, when I turned to my best man and said, *"There is no way that I am marrying some Christian female."*

He told me that I could leave now. The wedding has started, and then I said, *"Watch me,"* and I stepped off the platform. Just at that moment the organ played the bride's invocation, the doors opened in the back, and there stood Karen in her wedding dress, which I had not seen, with her father at her side. I looked at her, and knew I loved her. I stepped back onto the platform and told my best man, *"Now I am marrying her; she is just downright foxy!"*

So, we did get married, and it was good and hard all at the same time. I was now a husband, but I had no clue what that really was. But also, I became a father that day of a three-year-old boy, Scotty, and a one-year-old daughter, Sandy. To say the least, I was now in an "oppor-tunity" that I had never been in before, and in a very short time I was not handling things very well. For me, my wrestling match with God was still going on, and I struggled with going to church and commit-ting to God.

Many times Karen would ask me if I would like to go to church, and I would say no, so she would not go either. Her response to me was always respectful and kind, which would cause in me some pondering. Ever so often, on a Saturday night I would then ask Karen if she wanted to go to church, and her response 100 percent of the time was, "If you do."

I liked the tenderness I saw about her as we went to church, but unknowingly I was creating questions in Karen's mind about whether she was saved with things that I said. Because I had such a unique expe-rience with the Lord and the outpouring of that wind—an experience she didn't have—whenever she would do something that wasn't what I considered "Christian" or "good," I hypocritically ran her down and said it showed she wasn't really saved. (Never mind the things *I* was doing that weren't good or Christian!)

We were two misfits with a lot of issues—two people in love and being drawn in by God, but still very much messed up. We had hard times from the get-go, because while getting married is wonderful, you both bring into a marriage whatever baggage you're still carrying. We both had plenty, but God had drawn us together, and now He was drawing us to Himself.

Life was rough for a while. Anyone who tells you everything is perfect after you get saved is not giving you the truth, because we still live in a messed-up world full of messed-up people. Also, getting married will never solve all your problems. However, you do get to tackle your problems *together*, and when you're committed to working through them there's nothing better than having someone who loves you to pick you up when you fall.

Not terribly long after we got married, I lost my job roofing when the economy collapsed in California, and then I ended up making stupid choices and falling out of the back of a pickup while drunk after partying with some friends. That would give me a skull fracture. I "lost" three days and woke up on our couch with no memory of doctor visits at the VA. She told me all these horror stories I cannot remember to this day.

Worse, three months later, even after we'd decided to get our lives straightened out, we were in a head-on car accident on the Ventura freeway in the San Fernando Valley. We were in a 1970 Toyota Corolla, and a woman who was driving drunk in a 1963 Chevrolet Impala hit us head on. It absolutely ruined the day!

I had made it into the final five applicants to get onto the LAPD, (that is the Los Angeles Police Department) and the night of the accident we'd gone out dancing but I'd only had one beer. We were committing to going to church and doing things right, but this lady in an Impala didn't know that and crossed the median to collide with us head on!

Karen was hurt badly, and I woke up for a moment lying in the middle of the freeway. A fireman was at my left and a Highway Patrolman standing behind me and I said to them, "My wife!" I looked over and saw firemen bring my wife out of the car with a lot of her skin on her forehead hanging from her face, and then I passed out only to wake up in the hospital the next day. While we both eventually recovered, I was too banged up to pass the physical for the LAPD at that time and the job opportunity passed.

We lost our apartment because I still had no roofing work and didn't become a policeman, and so we moved in with my parents. Every newlywed's dream, right? It was not a high point for us, and I felt emotionally and mentally fatigued—recently married, Karen and two kids to support, and here we were back in the house with my parents. Truthfully it wasn't all that much fun for anybody.

So, when I heard that the construction business in Colorado Springs was booming, we decided I'd go out there to see if I could get a job. My friend Jack and I headed to Colorado, and we found jobs immediately. We worked for a month, and then I rented a duplex and drove back to California to get Karen, who was pregnant, and the kids. We packed up a U-Haul and headed to Colorado.

It was time for a new chapter in our lives—a better one, we hoped.

I was still struggling with God, but He knew what I needed. He provided a mentor for me in Colorado in the form of a man named Bill Hodges, a real man's man. I somehow met Bill in a hardware store, and we started up a conversation. Somewhere in that conversation, he told me that he was starting a church, and I asked him, "What does that mean?" I seemed to know by his confidence and demeanor that he was a man's man, and that was important to me. I would find out later that he had been a missionary in Brazil for twenty years.

I liked him personally; we started going to his church. Bill was a Baptist, and he gave an invitation for people to come up front to be prayed for or receive Jesus after every service. Then someone would come and usher those people into a small side room for more prayer or to talk.

I remember during one evening service, Bill had a special speaker, and after the man spoke, Bill got up and gave an invitation. I leaned over and told Karen, "There is no way in hell I'd walk up some aisle."

The next thing I knew, I was standing up there next to Bill!

I literally have no memory of getting up and walking up there, but suddenly I "woke up" standing in front of the whole church.

"What is it, Gus?" Bill asked me.

I was fighting through being disoriented at just ending up there in front of everyone, but then I said, "I think I want to surrender everything to the Lord. Surrender it all." I meant it, too—the anger, with life and with God, my confusion, my plan for my life—everything. I didn't care what it was; I wanted to just give it all to God.

"But I'm afraid," I whispered to Bill, "that I'm going to cry."

"It's okay," Bill told me, putting one arm over my shoulder. "Gus, good men do cry." This, coming from a man's man.

With that, I bowed my head before the Lord and said, "Father, I surrender to You and ask for forgiveness for all I've done in these years of anger. I want You alone, and I desire that Your will become my will. I want to be renewed in You."

I was sobbing and expected someone to come and take me to the side room where they'd pray for me. But nobody came, and instead Bill turned me around, and told the congregation to sit down.

"Gus has something to tell you," he said to them.

"Bill, you low lifer," I said. He just laughed.

But I faced the congregation, took a deep breath, and said, "I just surrendered my life and everything to the Lord, so from now on whatever I eat, whatever I drink, whatever I look at, whatever I listen to, or whatever I say will be for the glory of God."

Indeed, we'd turned to a new chapter in our lives. ·

I have no idea where the words I said that day came from. I had yet to read what the Apostle Paul wrote: *"So whether you eat or drink or whatever you do, do it all for the glory of God"* (1 Corinthians 10:31 NIV).

We all eventually come to a place in our faith where we must make a decision. The choice is this: Do I mean it, or not? Am I committed, or am I just pretending?

Christian-sounding words about faith and Jesus are all well and good, but God does not want what's called "lip service"—He wants our whole hearts. Lip service is where we say the right things, but we're not too interested in letting Him do a complete life makeover.

I want this to be clear: The message of grace means that you cannot white-knuckle your Christianity by trying hard and doing the right things. You can't discipline yourself into being a man or woman of God, because being a good Christian isn't about doing things—it's about *knowing Him and believing His Word about who you are in Jesus.* However, you cannot just lazily wander your way through your faith and expect to truly know God.

So, while we do not earn His love by doing the right things, our hearts come to a place where we must decide what kind of faith we want to live—the powerful kind that springs from knowing God, or the anemic kind that sounds good on a coffee mug or bumper sticker but offers no life change.

I had wrestled with God for years by the time I found myself walking forward at Bill's invitation. I was exhausted from the fight, and I was tired of being on the fence. There's one thing I can tell you about straddling the fence between being all-in for God and wanting to do your own thing; riding the fence *hurts*. It's not where you want to be. In fact, God wants us to be hot or cold—all-in or not—rather than on the fence.

For me, the time had come to decide. I was tired of being tired, so I surrendered to God. I wanted His will in my life, and I so wanted to know Him.

The thing is, when we surrender to God, *we do not lose*. It is only in surrendering to God that we truly *win*. I really found out that His Word is absolute truth. This is what He did in my life. "*And we know that God causes everything to work together for the good of those who love God…*" (Romans 8:28 NLT).

That's exactly what He did in our lives!

CHAPTER 13:

HUNGRY FOR THE LORD

I was all-in. Nothing was going to hold me back anymore. I'd received God's gift of grace in Jesus Christ as a seventeen-year-old teenager in Oregon; as a man, I surrendered to Him in Colorado. What's the difference, you might ask?

When we are children, we think as children do. We believe unflinchingly like children do (which God likes). We can encounter God, but often we aren't as emotionally mature as we might think we are. Then often "life happens" and knocks a lot of that childlike trust out of us. When we grow up a little more, we often find that we must surrender to God with an adult's understanding because life has gotten in the way and made us forget that childlike faith with God. The Lord wants us to recover our childlike joy and ability to trust in Him.

Life had gotten in my way. It had clouded the experience I had with His wind rushing through me that had renewed my spirit. Now, after having been angry with God and running from Him for years, I was ready to surrender all that I am to Him, mentally and emotionally.

One of the first signs that something had truly happened to me was that I became hungry—hungry for God's Word. Like that eager desire

I had to read the Gospel of John that I had as a teenager, I began consuming the Bible like a starving man diving into a feast.

Suddenly, because I drank so much in my past I didn't feel right about having a beer in my refrigerator (we put it under the sink at first). I quit smoking. In fact, I quit the next morning after I stood up in Bill's church. I didn't feel I could smoke for the Lord's glory, so I told Him, "God, I'm going to quit after I finish this pack of cigarettes."

I reached into my pocket…to find one cigarette left! As I said, God has a sense of humor.

So did Pastor Bill! He asked me to teach the teenagers the Word of God, which they called the youth group. For some reason, I said yes.

I remember the first night the kids came over. Two weeks had gone by since I had surrendered to God, and I was devouring His Word, but there was a lot I hadn't read yet. Remember, I'd only read John and Acts till that point. I asked the kids what they wanted to learn, and they said, "The rapture."

I had no idea what that was.

So, I grabbed my Bible and looked at the mini concordance in the back. I couldn't find "rapture" in there anywhere! I remember looking at Karen and asking, "What did we get into here, a cult?" So, we called Bill's wife, and she gave us the details.

Despite very humble beginnings, the group that started out with twelve kids turned into thirty-six after about three or four weeks. God just kept blessing it and blessing it, and I just talked about the only part of the Bible I knew anything about—the Gospel of John.

I asked Bill what else we should do with these kids, and he told me to take them "soul winning."

"Soul winning?" I asked. "What's that?"

Bill told me, "Everybody loves it when you knock on their doors and tell them about Jesus. They just love it!" He taught me to just walk up to a door, knock on it, introduce myself and one of the kids, and then ask them if we can talk about something—the Gospel. We'd share Jesus with them, and they'd love it.

So, I took him at his word, and we took the kids "soul winning." I told the kids how everyone would just love it when we knocked on their door and started witnessing to them about Jesus.

Thursday evening came, and I took one kid, Kevin, with me up to the first door while the others stayed back and watched. We knocked on the door, and this guy opened it. I introduced Kevin and myself and told him we were from Gideon Baptist Church and asked if he had a few minutes to answer a few questions.

The guy started cussing at us! He used every mean, dirty word in the book, and while I was used to them, I knew Kevin wasn't. The guy yelled at us to get off his blankety-blank porch and slammed the door!

I remember standing there looking at the door, being very concerned as to how the kids were feeling. So I just turned to the kids and told them, "That's not normal." So, we went on to the next house.

We walked over to the next house, knocked on the door, and a fragile little old lady answered. I was so stinking pumped; I thought this would go well for sure. I introduced Kevin and myself like before, and when she heard that we were from Gideon Baptist Church something happened in her.

She was the most foul-mouthed old woman I'd ever heard in my life! She started swearing at us in words I hadn't heard in a long time and threatened to call the police! She then slammed her door.

I walked back to the kids, and I told them, "As surely as there's a God in heaven, there's a Lucifer, and that's what this is—it's the devil!" That seemed about right. "What's going to happen tonight is that we're going after the souls of men for the glory of God! People are going to come to Christ, and we're going to go kick butt for the glory of God!"

We split up, and I can honestly say that those amazing teenagers led two families to the Lord that very night, despite the way it had started off so poorly. Two entire families ended up coming to God and then attending the church—mom, dad, and the kids—and they all got baptized!

It was such a thrill to see our kids out there. They'd taken a hit; they could've been discouraged and fearful. Instead, they stepped out in faith, and God showed up!

Bill heard about the results. "Gus, you've been called to the ministry," he told me.

I shook my head. "I'm not going into the ministry," I said to him. "I'm going to start my businesses and be a millionaire. I want to be an entrepreneur; I'm not going into no ministry. I have no desire to do that."

In fact, he was so persistent, and because I loved him too much to want to argue with him, I told Karen, "We're moving back to California!"

We'd been in Colorado just one year, but it was possibly the most pivotal year of my life.

We moved back with no job, new baby Danny, and Scotty and Sandy, whom I adopted in Colorado. I want to say something about the adoption that our Lord would use in our life forever. When we walked into the judge's chambers he said to me, *"Young man, do you know what you are doing?"* I was twenty-six years old and I told him, "Yes, I do." He said, *"If you adopt these children and then you two divorce each other you will pay child support."* I then said, "Why would we ever get divorced?" He then went on to say, *"If you adopt them you are not their stepfather and they are not your stepchildren; you are their father and they are your children and it will be so on their birth certificates. Also you can never change your mind; there is no such thing as coming here and un-adopting your children. Do you understand what I am saying?"* "Yes, I do, your honor. They are already my children." His words would bless me beyond measure when I read in God's Word, *"God decided in advance to adopt us into his own family by bringing us to himself through Jesus Christ. This is what he wanted to do, and it gave him great pleasure"* (Ephesians 1:5 NLT). I know what it means to have great pleasure in adopting and being adopted!

We also moved in with my parents again—all because I didn't want to be in the ministry and didn't want my friendship with Bill to end in a fight because I wouldn't do it.

Little did I know it wasn't *Bill* who wanted me in the ministry!

We went back to Allan's church. When he heard that I'd surrendered to God, he asked me to teach fifth grade. I asked him to teach me how to do evangelism like he did. So, he started teaching me how to lead people to Jesus in a variety of situations. I became passionate about it, and everywhere I went, I found people coming to Christ! I'd meet with Allan every Thursday night, and we'd go out together and talk to people about Jesus. It was absolutely wonderful.

I didn't understand that it wasn't *Bill* who was saying I was called to ministry, it was God, and the call was evident on my life. Allan perhaps knew me well enough not to say anything to my face right away; he just let the hunger drive me, and he simply instructed it and channeled it. I had no idea that God was preparing me for future ministry because at the time I wasn't open to it and was still pretty rough around the edges.

I didn't teach fifth graders long; Allan moved me up to junior high. I taught them the Gospel of John, which is basically the story of Jesus, and my goal was to make it real in their lives instead of forcing anything on them.

But I would not put up with disrespect. One kid, Bob, was typical of junior high boys. He'd sit in the back and just talk and talk. He was always sitting near these girls and interrupting, and over and over I told him to knock it off.

Finally, I'd had enough. I walked over to Bob and said, "Knock it off! One more time and I'm going to pick you up and throw you against the wall!"

Well, he must have thought I was joking. He did it one more time.

I walked back to where he was sitting, picking him up over my head, and threw him! He bounced off the ceiling, into the wall, and hit the floor. Then I picked him up, kicked open the door, and tossed him out!

I shut the door and walked back to the class. "Now, open your Bibles," I told them. They all jerked to respond; I had their attention! I was pumped; I thought we'd get some real Bible study done after that.

The pastor wasn't so pumped. Allan said, "Oh, great, we're going to get sued!"

"For what?" I asked. "He was constantly disrespectful and unruly!"

I had to promise not to throw anyone else against walls or out the door, and we didn't get sued. In fact, about a month later, there was a knock at the classroom door.

It was Bob.

"Can I come back to your class?" he asked meekly.

Bob came back, and he became an excellent student. In fact, years later he became a youth pastor! I'd hear the story from his perspective—watching me toss him like a giant and flying backward into the ceiling. We would laugh, and it brought me great joy to think of him as a youth pastor.

Maybe we all need a good tossing from time to time.

About the time Bob came back, Allan asked if I would go with him to a Navajo reservation in about six months to teach the Word of God. "Is this the kind of decision I'm supposed to pray about?" I asked him. He said it was, so I did—and Karen and I felt like God said, "Yes." So, I told Allan I'd go.

When we moved back to California, we moved back in with my parents. I was looking for a job, but months passed by. Things were tense because we had no money, and my parents couldn't take care of all of us. Finally, construction was starting up, and the guy I used to work for hired me back. We were doing what is called Cedar shake roofs, and I could make money doing that.

I'd been back to work for two weeks when Allan told me, "Gus, we're leaving for the Navajo reservation next week."

But I'd just gotten a job! I couldn't take off a week.

I remember thinking, "Wait a minute, God, I asked You about this! I prayed, and You said to go. You knew I was going to get this job, so how is this supposed to work?"

But God had told us I should go—Karen and I agreed on that. So, we decided that I could at least talk to the foreman and ask. I told him the whole story about agreeing to go six months ago, praying about it, and so forth. I ended with telling him that I understood—since I'd only been at work for two weeks—and if he said I couldn't go, I wouldn't go. No hard feelings.

"Yeah, you can go," the foreman told me. Then he cussed at me! "In fact, you can go anywhere you want. You're fired just for asking—get your tool box and get out of here!"

So, I went home to tell Karen. "He said I can go..." I told her.

"He did?"

"...And then he fired me just for asking!"

We couldn't believe it. Why was God doing this? But God had said I should go, so we were committed. My dad was furious—for me still wanting to go, and for me losing my job over it. "When you get back," he told me angrily, "your family will be out on the street! They will not be in this house."

I knew I was supposed to go, but did not know what to do with my family.

I told Allan all about it. He and his wife Nancy said to bring my family to their house. So, we moved into their place, and then we left for the reservation.

I spent a week teaching sixteen and seventeen-year-olds from the Gospel of John. They told me these kids wouldn't laugh, that they were straight-faced, and not to try to get them to show a lot of emotions because it was not their way to in front of strangers.

I didn't listen. My entire goal was to teach them the book of John...and to get them to laugh!

He wasn't kidding; I'd never seen a human being so stiff as these kids. But I was determined. The second day, in the morning this pretty little Navajo girl in the front half-smiled at something I said, and I knew I had her! I said, "I got you!" and as soon as I did, she started laughing—along with the rest of the class!

That was an amazing, transformative week. We stayed in this little class C motorhome, and I had to go pick the kids up in a 55 Chevy four-wheel drive truck. I got invited to many of their homes, which are called "hogans," with the families of the children I was teaching.

I remember dropping off the last child on the last day at the last hogan. I was out in the middle of nowhere, but I stopped the truck and got out. I lifted my arms in worship, and I said, "Father, I surrender again. If You want me in Your ministry, I will go!

I couldn't think of any greater joy than what I'd just experienced with those kids that week. I couldn't wait to tell Karen.

When I got back to California, I went to see if I could get my job back. It turned out that the foreman who fired me never worked there again; in fact, the whole housing tract went bankrupt. I would've lost my job regardless!

If I hadn't listened to God, I would've missed out on one of the best weeks of my life and the pivotal event that drew me into the ministry. When I went anyway, it felt like complete foolishness, but the foolishness of God is just a different type of wisdom—His type. It leads us to trust and faith in Him, which is the smartest thing of all.

I look back at all the mistakes and blunders I've made, like tossing junior high kids against ceilings and out the door (which I know so many junior high pastors have wanted to do!), and I'm amazed that God could use me anyway.

By every account, leaving my job after two weeks to teach God's Word at the reservation was another mistake, but it was one I made because God said so. When you decide to turn your life over to God, not everything He tells you to do will make sense. In fact, obeying Him can seem like a foolish mistake.

We read in 1 Corinthians 1:18, 24-25,

"The message of the cross is foolish to those who are headed for destruction! But we who are being saved know it is the very power of God.... But to those called by God to salvation, both Jews and Gentiles, Christ is the power of God and the wisdom of God. This foolish plan of God is wiser than the wisest of human plans, and God's weakness is stronger than the greatest of human strength" (NLT).

Human wisdom would say that going on a missions trip after being back at work for only two weeks was foolish. It would say I should stay home and take care of my family—that's what made sense there.

Except God had a different plan. His plan was deeper than our short-term financial comfort; He was setting me up for a life in His ministry. Going on that trip was the wisest thing I could ever have done because God told me to go and used it to direct the course of the rest of my life.

What "foolish" thing is God telling you to do right now? Something new and amazing may be just on the other side of your obedience. I dare you: Buy into God's wisdom, even if you've made mistakes before, and wait eagerly to see what He will do in your life.

"Delight yourself in the LORD and he will give you the desires of your heart" (Psalm 37:4 NIV 1984).

CHAPTER 14:

LEARNING ABOUT GOD

After my fantastic week with the Navajo kids and surrendering to God's call to the ministry, it was incredible how things began to click. I didn't even fully understand what it meant to be "in the ministry," but I began to admit to people that God wanted me to do it, and I was more than willing.

Seeing that I now had a direction, my parents allowed us to move back in while I looked for a job. Karen and I prayed, and in no time I started a new roofing job, and then after a month of looking for a house to rent, we suddenly found one whereas before we could not find anything available.

However, the roofing job was not the answer to our prayers. Though it was owned by a man from the church, it was unstable and barely enough to pay the bills. When a guy named Bill called me one night and asked if I was looking for work, I told him yes.

He asked, "Have you ever thought about being a milkman?" A milkman? I told him I hadn't. He went on, "I am looking for a man to work with me. So would you at least look at it?" I said yes and asked about time and place. He told me the place and said the time was 2:00 a.m. That was a *wow* for me.

The job was delivering Laurel Wood Acres Goat milk and Alta Dena milk to Ralph's supermarkets in the Los Angeles basin, and to my joy the milk truck was a five-ton Bobtail. Plus, I found out later that the early schedule would allow me flexibility for school.

I was in!

The amusing thing was that Bill was the husband of the woman who told me to get out of there the first time I visited Allan's church after returning from Vietnam. You may remember that I also said God used me to lead their son to surrender his whole life to Christ when he was in the eleventh grade, so it is interesting to see how God turned that initial poor first impression to our good and His glory.

With our financial needs taken care of, it was time to go on to the next step. Allan told me I needed to go to college. Since Allan was a Baptist, you might expect that he would recommend a Baptist college, but instead, he recommended Life Bible College. I didn't know anything about denominational divisions within the Church, which didn't give me any prejudices against Pentecostalism.

I dove right into Life, and I was lucky that my work at the dairy allowed me to be flexible. I worked from 4:00 a.m. to 2:00 in the afternoon. But I had to be at school from 7:00 till 10:00 p.m. It was a one-hour motorcycle ride from our house to Life Bible College, so I had a full schedule working full time and going to school full time.

It was a blast!

By my third week, the teacher, along with some of the students, decided that they were going to pray for me that I would be filled with the Holy Spirit with the evidence of speaking in tongues (but I didn't know that). We bowed our heads to pray in my English class, and suddenly somebody grabbed my head and started shaking it! Hands were all over me, and the old angry me just about jumped up and hit someone!

But I quickly thought, "Father, they love You a lot, so they're trying to do good." Thankfully, I didn't hit any of them!

They prayed for me for about two hours. We didn't have class that night. They prophesied over me and said that my gift would reach tens of thousands of people and that I would have an apostolic gift. I didn't know what that was, and I couldn't even picture many thousands of individuals, but I knew that they were sincere in their prayers and I responded with an Amen!

There was an overwhelming presence of the Holy Spirit that night, and He gave gifts to me as it pleased Him, but not the gift of tongues. From then on, I was known as a "Baptecostal!"

I later invited Karen to come with me to an evening class taught by Pastor Jack Hayford, an amazing and gifted teacher in the Los Angeles area. I was excited for her to hear him, but the entire time Karen was wondering if they were going to "assault" her in prayer as they had me! She was jumpy the whole time, but we thoroughly enjoyed hearing this incredible teacher in person.

I spent two years at Life Bible College, and I loved it. I learned Greek and Hebrew, and I was a good student. I would've stayed, except that we had a difference of doctrinal belief regarding whether you can lose your salvation. Unfortunately, they wanted me to sign a document that I believed this particular doctrinal point as they did, but I could not do it, so I left.

Many years after, on our twenty-fifth wedding anniversary, we went to see Allan at the church in the little town he was pastoring in Arizona. I asked him, "I've always wondered and never asked you why you wanted me to go to Life Bible College instead of a Baptist college. Why did you do that?"

He said one of the most beautiful things: "I wanted you to know that God is bigger than being a Baptist, and I knew you'd find your way. You needed to hear more."

After leaving Life Bible College, I was interested in attending a Bible college in Phoenix, Arizona, so a friend of mine, Bob, (who also went to the Navajo reservation with us) and I went out there to check it out. He and his wife had both been divorced before they met and got married. Then they both received God's gift of grace in Jesus the Christ. When we met with the president of the college, we made sure to tell him Bob and his wife's story. Because that was a big deal in certain denominations, being divorced, we wanted to make sure that it was not going to be an issue at this Bible college, and the president assured us that it would not be a problem.

It seemed like a great opportunity, and Bob and I moved our families out to Phoenix. I found work as a roofer, and Bob got a job as a glazier at a glass company.

However, no sooner did we get there to start school than they told Bob that he could not take Bible courses there because he had been divorced! We had already moved our families, but apparently they had reversed their position. I left that school out of principle, but we were now in Phoenix, and I was questioning whether or not I wanted to be in the ministry if it meant dealing with things like this.

Fortunately, the pastor of the church, Chuck Vaden, where we were attending liked me and saw the call of God on me. He asked me if I would be willing to start a college ministry for their church of about eight hundred people. Out of the hundreds of people attending, they only had seven college students. But they gave us a back room to meet in, and somewhere around ninety days later God had multiplied seven college students into one hundred! We couldn't even fit them all in one room.

The pastor saw the way God was using us and told me he thought I was called to the ministry. This time, however, I replied, "I thought about that, but I don't know...." After my bad experience with a Bible college, I wasn't sure.

He said, "I think there is a school you should go to. It's called Pacific Coast Baptist Bible College."

"Where's that?" I asked.

"San Dimas, California," he replied. "But I just came from California!" I said.

We decided to move back to Southern California and attend the Baptist college, but they would not accept any of my two years of credits from Life Bible College—none of them. So I made a decision, and I took a heavy class load of twenty-four credits a semester because I wanted to get done quickly. I was back at work at the dairy, where they were surprisingly understanding and allowed me the flexible schedule to attend college.

I got A's in every class because I was totally consumed with the things of God. But I realized that while I was learning things about God, I wasn't getting any closer to God. I was gaining the knowledge and academics, but I had been more intimate in my relationship with the Lord before I got that knowledge.

With the heavy course load and working full time, my schedule was very demanding. I was either at work or school most of every day, and I gave Karen half an hour every evening from 9:00 to 9:30 p.m. to talk about anything she wanted—but when the half hour was up, we were done, and I went to study!

I had a deep yearning in my soul and told God about it. "I'm not getting closer to You," and I felt like He was urging me to draw near to Him again. But I told Him, "I don't have any time!" I kept feeling Him nudge me to spend time with Him, and I did not want to say to the Lord I would do something but not do it. The only thing I could do was get up earlier, and I was going to bed after midnight every day. So one day I said to the Lord, "I will get up at 5:00 in the morning instead of 5:30 so I can spend time with You."

I had an aggressive reading plan that included two chapters out of various portions of the Bible, and I read two chapters from each section every day, out loud.

At first, the reduced sleep was brutal. I was nearly falling asleep on the freeway! However, after about ten days it began to get better and better. Within three or four months, I was getting up at 3:30 in the morning to spend time with God and His Word, and I was more alive than I had ever been!

But while I was doing all this, Karen was struggling with her salvation. It was a problem that would have dire consequences for us later.

One morning our Lord did something that would flat out overwhelm me. I was reading about twenty-five chapters a morning from His Word and then praying from thirty to forty-five minutes. On that morning after reading His Word, I felt that I needed to lie on the floor and began to worship our Lord.

I am not sure how to explain this, but our Lord's presence came into the room that morning with bright glory, overwhelming love, joy, and fear all at the same time. When I felt Him lifting me off the floor, I shouted, "STOP!" He did, which I have always regretted. I said "stop" because I was concerned for Karen who was struggling with her salvation.

At the frantic pace I was going, I was set to graduate in a year. But I knew something wasn't right. What would it mean for me to graduate? What was "the ministry" anyway? Where was I supposed to go? What was I expected to do? I didn't know, but I wanted to find out.

So one morning I told Karen, "I'm going to the desert."

"What are you going to do?" she asked.

"I'm going to meet with the Lord," I told her. She asked when I would come home. I told her, "I may never come home. If God doesn't meet with me, He knows He is going to have a dead carcass on His hands. I'm not coming back if He doesn't meet with me. He's got to tell me what to do." Looking back, I can't imagine what Karen must've been thinking and feeling!

I took my .357 magnum Python revolver for snakes, a lot of water, our dog Heidi, and food for the dog. Of course, I also brought my Bible. I drove out to the Mojave Desert, slept that first night, and got up in the morning to meet with the Lord. I prayed, "I know You know that I'm here. And You know that I'm not leaving until You meet with me. I need to know what I am supposed to be doing!"

I spent all day reading the Bible, starting in Matthew and reading out loud and talking about the things I read with the Lord. I drank water, fed and watered our dog, and just kept going. The next day was the same thing.

Sometime around 11:00 a.m. that morning, I felt the presence of the Lord come! When He came, I hit the ground faster than I could believe possible. There was a light, and joy, and fear that were overwhelming!

The Lord spoke to me audibly,

He proceeded to tell me what I would be doing. He told me who I would work for, and that I would never graduate with an academic degree. He said my only boast would be in Him all the days of my life and that He would never let me retire. "I will be your retirement," the Lord told me.

I listened to it all lying on the ground as God painted the broad scope and the details, all of it.

When I got up I found my dog, Heidi, about a half mile away. We walked back to the van, drove to a pay phone in Mojave, and called Karen. "I met with the Lord, and you won't believe it, He spoke to me out loud!" I told her. I couldn't wait to share all of it with her.

I was starving, so I bought a hamburger, but then suddenly I wasn't hungry at all. I had filled up on the joy of the Lord.

As we grow in the Lord, it's easy to replace the first relational connection we have with Him with intellectual knowledge of God. The same way we can forget our childlike faith and trust in Him, we can think knowing more *about God* is the same as *knowing God better*. But that is not always the case!

It's easy to get lost in the "doing" of faith and lose sight of the "being"—just being with God for the sake of getting to know Him better. If you wanted to know your spouse better, would you pick up their biography and read about them, or would you spend time in their presence? If you want to know someone, you do not need knowledge only; you need time spent together.

Jesus revealed many things to the Apostle John while he was in exile on the island of Patmos. He wrote the book of Revelation from these things, and it included messages from Jesus to specific churches of the era. One was to the church in Ephesus, and in his letter to this church, Jesus told John that He recognized the things that they did. He saw their hard work and patient endurance and that they had suffered for Him without quitting.

But then He said this: *"Yet I hold this against you: You have forsaken the love you had at first. Consider how far you have fallen! Repent and do the things you did at first..."* (Revelation 2:4-5a NIV).

Notice the beginning: They had forgotten their first love. Could this describe your walk with God? Have you substituted head knowledge of God for passionately knowing Him?

God is a jealous God, and He wants our hearts—in fact, He wants all of us like a lover! He does not just want us to have intellectual knowledge of Him; He wants us to want to *know Him!*

If your love has grown cold or stale, I encourage you to repent as your act of worship and do what you did at first. Return to the early ways in which you loved God and came to know Him, how He drew you to Himself. Ask Him to woo you back, for He is the great love of our lives, and there is nothing better than knowing Him!

CHAPTER 15:

A SMALL CHANGE OF PLANS

When I got back from the desert, I told Karen that God told me I was going to work for Pastor Chuck Vaden. She immediately replied, "If you're supposed to work for Chuck, maybe you should call him."

I said, "If I'm supposed to work with Chuck Vaden, God can tell him. Because I'm not going to call him. God said to me I'm working with Chuck Vaden. If God tells me I'm working with Chuck Vaden, I'm working with Chuck Vaden. *He'll* call *me!*"

I went out into the desert in September. Early in December of that year, I got a call from Chuck. "Hey Gus, what are you doing on New Year's Eve?" he asked.

"Nothing, but I have to work New Year's Day for the dairy," I replied.

"Good," he said. "I'll let you out at midnight."

"From what?"

Chuck told me, "I want you to preach for me at our New Year's Eve service."

In Phoenix. An eight-hour drive from Los Angeles. "I'll do it!" I told him.

It was a blast! True to his word, Chuck walked us out to our car right at midnight. As Karen was getting in the car, he said, "Gus?" I looked up. "I want to ask you something. Would you consider coming on as my associate pastor?" he asked.

"Aren't I supposed to pray about that or something before I answer?" I asked with a smile.

I told him I would call him in a week, but as soon as we were in the car and driving away, Karen and I began shouting in excitement. I can't even describe the joy it was for us to have him confirm what God had told me in the desert.

I went back and finished school, and I graduated but with no degree because I had yet to finish summer school. We went back and rented a house in Phoenix, and I started working on summer school in California. I would go home on the weekends. Everything looked like it was going to work out perfectly.

But perhaps you have learned that things rarely work out "perfectly"—or at least the way we expect them to.

Around the first of August, I was finished with school and was able to move back to Phoenix with my family. In the middle of August Chuck Vaden and his family took off in their small plane—he was an excellent pilot—and headed to Ohio where he's from. On the way back, their plane got caught in a thunderstorm in the panhandle of Texas. On that day, the thunderstorm took their plane down!

It was a horrible tragedy—his married daughter, his teenage son, his beautiful wife, and himself, all killed instantly. At that time, it was the largest funeral in the state of Arizona, with six thousand people in attendance.

He had intended to introduce me to the deacons and staff of the church when he returned from vacation. He had told them that he was going to hire me, but he had not yet told them for what. He never told them that I was going to be the new associate pastor, and of course, he never came back.

I knew and was friends with the deacons and staff at the church, and they were good men. They all liked me, and I liked them. But suddenly without Chuck telling them how I would fit in the church, I was for all purposes set aside and had nothing to do.

It was our second trip to Phoenix that felt stillborn and like a tragic misunderstanding. Had the accident taken God by surprise? Of course not. Was it part of His plan? I couldn't see how. I felt like a leaf spinning in the wind, out of control and uncertain despite the clear words from God I had received in the desert.

I knew our Lord had brought me there, but now I had no idea why.

I didn't know it at the time, but I was also encountering the political undercurrents of the church for the first time. Chuck did not consult with the church leadership on decisions or ask permission for anything, so they had no idea why he had hired me. They presumed that I was to be some type of missionary intern. I told them what Chuck had said to me, but nobody was listening because emotions were so high. Also, all the pastors on staff were "assistant pastors," and Chuck had intended for me to be an "associate pastor," which was a higher position. They certainly were not going to do that without Chuck telling them.

Without clear direction from church leadership, I was on my own. I started doing evangelism on Thursday nights leading people to Jesus, and I had to create things to keep myself busy in the broom closet office they gave me. I resumed the college ministry, and it started growing again, but I had no idea what God had thought when He told me I would work for Chuck.

They eventually hired a new pastor from the Huntington Beach, California, area. He had led the church of about a thousand people, and he came on the job after I had been there about a year. It had been a long year!

The new pastor decided to take the staff on a retreat, and we were going to plan the next year of ministry. He had a lot of big ideas to bring people into the church, such as bringing in Ronald McDonald the clown and feeding five thousand people fish sandwiches. He wanted to have pony rides, and when he found out that I used to own horses, I got saddled with that. When he found out that I jumped out of airplanes in Vietnam, he wanted me to get a permit and skydive from a plane and land in the parking lot!

"That will really bring the crowds in!" he said.

It was also at that meeting that this new pastor told us he was going to do something about the head deacon and called him something crude.

I was no stranger to rough language, but I knew those words were not to the glory of God. I came home and told Karen that I had never been to a meeting like that my whole life. "We didn't talk about Jesus, and we didn't speak about the Word," I said. I told her that all we had talked about was stupid big Sundays to get people to come in and visit the church.

"What are you going to do?" she asked.

I told her, "I'm going to get myself fired tomorrow."

The pastor had a huge office, and it was beautiful and well appointed. He had a bit of a belly on him, and he crossed his arms over his stomach and sat behind his big desk. He never came in before 10:00 a.m. I knew that because I was always there at 7:30 in the morning, typically an hour and a half before anybody else, meeting with the Lord and praying through the building.

When the pastor came in, I asked if I could see him. He called me in, and I quickly shared my story with him. God had been teaching me a lot about grace, and so I was very respectful. Then I got into the meat of it:

"You are meant to be the man of God," I told him. "I want to talk about the events. Feeding five thousand fish sandwiches is not why we are here. The Bible talks about making disciples," I told him. I then mentioned some Scriptures I had been reading about discipleship and how we are to set an example as we follow God so that people can be imitators of us as we imitate God.

"I'm not going to do pony rides," I said, "and I'm not jumping out of an airplane. And when you called the head deacon a crude word, that was wrong. I know that language; I was in the United States Marine Corps. I'm not offended by the word; I'm saddened by your actions when speaking of a man of God who is probably trying to do his best."

Remember, I was an intern.

"Are you finished?" he asked.

"I guess I am," I answered. I turned around and walked out and went home immediately, thinking that I had just gotten myself fired.

I went back into the office the next morning at 7:30, expecting that I would clear my stuff out of the closet office and be looking for a job the rest of the day. However, to my surprise, as I pulled in I saw the pastor's car was already in the parking lot. The way the parking lot was designed, the pastor's office would not permit him to see that it was me coming in, but as soon as he heard the door shut, the pastor said, "Gus, come on in here."

I walked into his grand office, and he just looked at me for a moment. "I want to tell you something," he said. "I didn't sleep last night. No one in my whole life has ever talked to me like you did."

I waited for the shoe to drop. "Here it comes…" I thought.

"Thank you."

It was not what I expected him to say!

"I want you to know, first of all, I already called the chairman of the deacons and apologized to him for what I said in front of you all," he told me. "I asked him to forgive me, and he has. I will get with the rest of the staff today and apologize to them as well. We're canceling everything today, and we're going to go back up to the retreat center in the mountains and will stay there and seek God till He tells us how in the world we are supposed to make disciples."

And that's exactly what we did.

We tried a variety of discipleship ministries, generally involving small groups. We tried different sizes and all kinds of other things, but mostly in people's houses. The plan was that after several months we would see what worked best. However, the key component of it all was seeking God and knowing Him. We all desired that His breath would become our own, and His Word would become ours. We sought to encourage others to want the same things.

The next thing you know, we were making disciples every which way. At one point, I squeezed seventy-five college age kids into my house! I was so happy! (But sixteen kids made for better discipleship.) We called our small groups "growth groups" in those days.

A couple of years passed. Discipleship was going well, and I loved teaching the college classes, though I didn't preach. However, the pastor was dealing with severe allergy problems, and they would present me with an opportunity to change the fact I wasn't yet a preacher.

One Sunday after the first service, where I taught the college class, I was walking into the main service just as the pastor was walking out. As I passed him, he said, "Gus, take it."

I stopped. "Take what?"

He didn't say anything. He just walked out the door. I followed him out as he headed for his car, but he got in and drove off before I could catch up!

I walked back into my office and grabbed my Bible. "Father," I prayed, "You said to be ready in any season. Now, it's the season—let's rock and roll!"

The worship was in full swing when I walked in the side door of the sanctuary. The pastor's chair was obviously empty, and I went and sat in it, which is what you're supposed to do if you're preaching. The other pastor gave me a meaningful look; it was go time.

I honestly have no memory of what I preached that day. It may have been out of Matthew (you were expecting John, perhaps?), and it was customary at our church to give an invitation at the end of the service.

"If you would like to receive the grace of God in Jesus Christ," I said in conclusion, "we ask you to come forward this morning."

As soon as I said that, some twenty to thirty people came rushing forward! I was completely stunned. We struggled to get enough people up front to help them all; it was unlike anything we ever saw on a Sunday.

When the pastor heard about it, he met with me and told me, "Gus, God has given you a call to preach."

Apparently He had!

I never wanted to preach and pastor a church. I went to Bible College for missions work, which I loved—leading people to Jesus. I love Him so much; it's easy for me to invite others to love Him too. It's just natural.

Leading a group of stiff-necked Christians in a church, with all the politics, differences of opinion, church government issues, and all the rest had never appealed to me. And as much as I enjoyed teaching the Word of God, I enjoyed preaching it.

However, my pastor was right—God had put an anointing on me to preach. I had my plans and preferences, but God had something else in mind.

That is how it often is. We frequently think we know how things should work out, and we can get angry or frustrated or disappointed when they don't go according to our plans. Sometimes this is because the world just isn't fair, but sometimes it's because God has a different plan for our lives.

God has good plans for our lives—plans to prosper us and not to harm us, plans that will give us hope and a future (see Jeremiah 29:11). We can either accept those plans, though we may not understand them, or we can fight them.

I had surrendered to God in Colorado, but I was working out, step by step, what that surrender looked like and entailed. Over and over, I thought I knew what God was doing...only to find out that I didn't know what He was doing in the details of my life. But when He revealed His way, it always brought me joy!

Proverbs 3:5-6 says, *"Trust in the Lord with all your heart, and lean not on your own understanding; in all your ways acknowledge Him, and He shall direct your paths."*

It's not that we should not make plans; we should. When we submit them to God, rather than relying on our own understanding, He directs our steps.

And His plans are *always* better. No matter what life throws at us, He will weave it together for our good. When we seek Him first, we set ourselves up to succeed—not at our plans, but at His. And whatever that may look like, I will take success at God's plans—even if it looks like failure and confusion to the world—than everything going right on my very best five or ten-year plan.

"Our Father in heaven, hallowed be your name, your kingdom come, your will be done..." (Matthew 6:9-10 NIV). This is the nature of surrender.

CHAPTER 16:

FAMILY MATTERS

There is no one like our Lord! When you are overwhelmed with Him, you will be filled with joy in the way He works within your family.

A couple of family stories stand out that I want to share with you. One is when Karen's grandfather, Dean, had a severe stroke when I was in my last year at Pacific Coast Bible College in California. While Karen was not all that close to her parents, she really loved Grandpa Dean.

It was a severe stroke, and they moved Dean from up in Lancaster, California, down to the Fullerton area, where they put him in a rehabilitation center. They had to tie him to his bed or to his wheelchair to prevent him from falling out, and his tongue hung out of the left side his mouth. They diapered and fed him like a baby, because he was unable to do a thing for himself, and we were told he would never leave that place.

The thought came to us that while that may be true, he still had breath, and God's Word can make a difference while someone still has breath. So, we decided to read the living Word of God to Him. As you might imagine, we read the Gospel of John. Why, you may ask? Because the Holy Spirit had a clear purpose for John writing it. John 20:30-31 says, "*Jesus did many other miraculous signs in the presence of his disciples, which are not recorded in this book. But these are written that you may believe that Jesus is the Christ, the Son of God, and that by believing you may have life in his name"* (NIV 1984).

Grandpa was a Mormon, as were many people on Karen's side of the family. Though they were not all practicing Mormons, it was a deeply rooted family tradition. Without getting into the weeds of Christianity versus Mormonism, we knew Grandpa likely did not have a personal relationship with Jesus Christ.

So, Karen and I took turns visiting Grandpa Dean. They would get Grandpa out of his bed, put something on him, get him into his wheelchair, and wheel him to the garden area where we would read the Gospel of John to him out loud. We did this for perhaps a month, going every other day and reading to him. One day Karen would go and the next time I would go. Several times we took our children along to enjoy Grandpa, even in his condition.

He never changed while we were there. Every time we visited, he looked unconscious. His tongue would hang out of his mouth, and we would see no response. But we would come back the next time and do it again.

One day, we had a family outing planned, but Karen woke up feeling like she needed to see her grandpa that day. "You take the kids, Gus," she told me.

When Karen walked into Grandpa's room, he was lying in bed, but he was mentally alert! This was the first time he had been like this since the stroke. Karen said, "Grandpa, I wanted to come see how you're doing. We've been praying for you. We've been reading the Bible to you, and I'm so glad you can hear what I'm saying today because I felt like God wanted me to talk to you about your relationship with Him." She began sharing the Gospel with him, and she finally asked if he knew Jesus personally or not.

"Oh," Grandpa said, "I want to know the Lord."

Though many in Karen's family were "Jack Mormons" (backslidden Mormons no longer living it), in his later years her grandfather had been going to the Mormon Church more than ever. But whatever it was he had been seeking in Mormonism, he had not found it.

It was Jesus Christ who said in Matthew 4:4, *Man does not live on bread alone, but on every word that comes from the mouth of God"* (NIV 1984). On that day, Grandpa received God's Word and became very much alive. He would tell me later that when Karen walked into his room, it was as if light was shining out of her. When she spoke, her words seemed to be *living.*

Karen stayed in the room with him, just praising God for what He had done, and she could not wait to get home to tell me. Sometime later that afternoon, Karen got a call from her mother. "What did you do to your grandfather?" her mom asked, like something was wrong.

"I talked to him about the Lord, and we read Scriptures," Karen told her. "He called on the name of the Lord today, and he became a Christian, a man of God!"

"Well, I don't know what you did, but he's like a totally different person!" her mom said. "He's alert, he's talking, and it's like he's back to normal."

Three days later, Grandpa went home. He was never supposed to leave that nursing center, but instead, he not only returned to live in his own apartment, but he also became an unbelievable evangelist for Christ! Grandpa lived the last six years of his life for Jesus, and it was nothing short of a miracle.

But the story doesn't end there. When Grandpa eventually passed away six years later, the family wanted him to be buried in Provo, Utah, so off we went to Provo for the funeral. Many in the family had gathered, both practicing Mormons and backslidden ones. Decked out in all his official robes, a Bishop of the Mormon Church and professor at Brigham Young University was to perform the service.

Karen's mother came up to me and said, "Gus, aren't you like a preacher or something?"

"Mom, I'm definitely something!" I told her.

"Well, we want you to say something at the end," she said. I told her I would.

The Bishop droned on and conducted the service with great gravity and nobility, but I felt like God wanted to do something. I got up to finish the service as I was asked by Karen's mom, and I felt inspired to read from Isaiah. I started by saying, "If Grandpa could come back today and speak to us from what he now sees, I am sure this is what he would say:

> "'You are my witnesses,' declares the LORD, 'and my servant whom I have chosen, so that you may know and believe me and understand that I am he. Before me no god was formed, nor will there be one after me. I, even I, am the LORD, and apart from me there is no savior.... Yes, and from ancient days I am he. No one can deliver out of my hand. When I act, who can reverse it?... I, even I, am he who blots out your transgressions, for my own sake, and remembers your sins no more.... This is what the LORD says—Israel's King and Redeemer, the LORD Almighty: I am the first and I am the last; apart from me there is no God. Who then is like me? Let him proclaim it.... You are my witnesses. Is there any God besides me? No, there is no other Rock; I know not one.... This is what the LORD says—your Redeemer, who formed you in the womb: I am the LORD, the Maker of all things, who stretches out the heavens, who spreads out the earth by myself.... I am the LORD, and there is no other; apart from me there is no God. I will strengthen you, though you have not acknowledged me, so that from the rising of the sun to the place of its setting people may know there is none besides me. I am the LORD, and there is no other.... For this is what the LORD says—he who created the heavens, he is God; he who fashioned and made the earth, he founded it; he did not create it to be

empty, but formed it to be inhabited—he says: 'I am the LORD, and there is no other.... Was it not I, the LORD? And there is no God apart from me, a righteous God and a Savior; there is none but me. Turn to me and be saved, all you ends of the earth; for I am God and there is no other.... Remember the former things, those of long ago; I am God, and there is no other; I am God, and there is none like me....' Our Redeemer—the LORD Almighty is his name—is the Holy One of Israel" (Isaiah 43:10-11,13,25; 44:6-8,24; 45:5-6,18,21-22; 46:9; 47:4 NIV).

I finished up by saying, "Amen!" And then I sat down.

The service was supposed to be over, but the entire time I quoted from Isaiah, the Bishop was getting angry. He looked at me like someone who hated me, and when I was finished, he got up and brought the book of Mormon and Pearl of Great Price with him to refute what I just said.

However, on this day God was not going to allow it. The Bishop opened his mouth to say something, but nothing but gibberish came out of his mouth. He tried again, looking confused...again nothing but gibberish! He looked stunned that he could not form any words, only sounds came out. So he folded up both books and walked out the back.

That day, God said, "No!"

Cousins that we had not seen in years came up to talk to us. Many of Karen's "Jack Mormon" relatives had come to know Jesus. "We loved your preaching," one said.

I said, "I didn't preach, I read the Scriptures!" It was not my words, they were God's words. The Bishop got up to refute me, but it wasn't me, it was God and His Word.

My Grandfather Trygve was one of those grandpas that every grandson wished he had. When I was growing up in Hawaii, my grandpa would pick me up and take me to Waikiki Beach so I could surf. He taught me a lot about driving and always had encouraging words for me. I knew I was loved by my grandpa.

When I graduated from Pacific Coast Bible College, my grandpa Trygve and Grandma Louise on my mom's side flew in from Hawaii for my graduation. Right after I had received my diploma, the president of the college said, "If there are any grandparents here who would like to present the diploma to their grandchild, please come up." My grandpa was so disappointed that they waited until after my diploma to mention it. But tomorrow morning was coming and our Lord had a great surprise for us all.

That morning my Grandpa Trygve sat down with me at the kitchen counter and said, "Gus, the reason I came to your graduation is that I want to know the Jesus that you know." That was the first time anyone had said, "I want to know the Jesus that you know."

Right there in my parents' kitchen, my grandfather received the overwhelming grace of the Almighty!

While we were living in Phoenix many years later, I got the call that Grandpa was in critical condition and to come as quickly as I could. It was a ridiculous price for an emergency ticket from Phoenix all the way to Hawaii, but we paid it so I could get there. I was on a United Airlines DC-10, which of course had different seating sections, but I was the only one flying in the middle coach section.

Just as the plane was getting ready to leave, this beautiful woman came to the door of the aircraft. At this time, there was less security, so a crying man was there, walking her right to the door. He kissed her and hugged her, sobbing, but she just looked at him as she got on the plane and he headed back. Her assigned seat? Right next to me, of course!

I was about thirty years old and happily married, and she was a beautiful woman in her mid-twenties, so it was a little awkward. The stewardess thought we were a couple!

However, being the outgoing person that I am, I started talking to her. I found out that the guy who had kissed her and was crying was her husband. She was leaving him to go to her boyfriend in Hawaii.

God was all over that situation, however. In probably just over an hour, she accepted Christ! Our Lord was in every detail of this event. The plane was taxiing down the runway to take off. They revved up the engines, and we were halfway down the runway, when they throttled back. The pilot got on the intercom and said that there was a mechanical problem and we had to go back to the main gate. That's how we had an hour.

That was awesome; instead of five hours of discipleship time, I would now have more! I took the opportunity and opened the Word of God and read to her from the Scriptures. It was incredible to see what happened to that woman's face! There was such transformation. I discipled her the entire flight to Hawaii, and by the time we landed, she was determined to drop the boyfriend, buy a return ticket, and go right back home to her husband.

As I exited the plane, I happened to see the boyfriend zooming in, trying to grab her and kiss her. Instead, she turned her head aside, and the last time I saw her she was unresponsive to his hug and looking back at me, with both her hands she gave me two thumbs up.

By the time I arrived in Hawaii, my grandpa had already died. He was in the presence of the Lord, whom he loved. I was drained, but I was proud to do his funeral. However, it was sad to look out and see so many members of that side of our family who did not know Jesus. It was hard to want to celebrate my grandfather's life and that he had passed into eternity with God when so few shared that bright hope.

Exhausted, I got back on another airplane and headed home. On my flight from LA to Phoenix, they sat me in the very last row of the plane, right next to the grumpiest-looking old man I'd ever seen. I remember praying, "Father, I don't care if he goes to hell, I don't want to talk to him." I was just so tired and worn out!

As we were taking off, he asked, "What do you do?"

I told him I taught—universities, marriage classes, and college classes. I finally admitted, "I also speak at churches."

"Oh, you're one of those!"

I turned to this man who seemed to just have a natural frown on his face and said, "No, I'm not one of those! I'm a man who ought to go to hell if God is just."

"I don't believe in hell," he said.

I turned to him and said, "That's not going to mean diddly-squat when you get there!"

As I said those words, we heard an explosion, and it felt like the tail of the airplane blew off! All the lights went off. The plane began wavering up and down, and then there was another explosion!

The pilot announced, "We've had a major malfunction and will be crash landing at LAX in fifteen minutes, so get prepared!"

I spent the next fifteen minutes telling that grumpy old man about Christ. He said he had been in World War II, and he felt like God had been trying to get his attention for some time.

"Are you ready to receive Him or not?" I asked him. For some reason, I felt I was to tell him this would be the last time the Holy Spirit would come and knock at the door of his heart.

We were landing, and this guy was glued on to me. I told him, "I am not your Savior! You're not going where I'm going."

We hit the runway with a boom, unsure what to expect. But the plane touched down okay, we were still alive, and the pilot got on to tell us they were going to taxi over to the gate to let us off. We got to the gate, and then suddenly the plane caught fire! The smoke was so bad, it was sucking the air out of our lungs and we had to get off by crawling out of the airplane.

I just wanted to get home, but they kept us cooped up in a room to keep us away from reporters so we wouldn't say anything. We also couldn't call anybody, so there was nothing to do for hours and hours. We all smelled horrible from the smoke from the electrical fire. But it was in that room that the grumpy old man received God's grace in Jesus Christ.

When I finally got back to Karen and the kids, they were so tired. The airline had not told anyone what had happened, so the flight was just listed as "delayed," keeping them in suspense the whole time.

When I got off the plane, Karen asked me what had happened. "Honey," I said, "they will never use that airplane again! It melted."

It's so strange that our own families can be the most challenging missions field for us. No one knows your dirty laundry like family. For those of you just coming to God, your family will know all the ungodly things you've done and may remind you of them. For all of you who've walked with God a long time…your family will know all the ungodly things you've done, too, and will sometimes not let you live it down!

However, just as we can be in a position of vulnerability to our family, we can also be in a position of transparency to them. We can let them see how we handle our sins and mistakes and still turn to God, and we can continually pray that the Lord will use us to be a witness to them through the very same oh-so-daily grind that also lets them see all our flaws and our new life in Christ.

There is no more important mission field than the home front. Paul tells Timothy that those who don't care for their families are denying the true faith, and Paul makes a point repeatedly that church leaders should be good at managing their own homes. This alone should tell us how important our families are to God, but the Word of God is full of how important family is.

CHAPTER 17:

UNDONE

I worked with Pastor Thomas Ray in Phoenix for just shy of three years, and during that time God took us all on a wonderful journey. Over those years, we saw hundreds of people come to Christ, and there was a spirit of joy seemingly from all directions of ministry.

One day, he told me, "Gus, you have a gift for church planting."

"I do?" I asked. "What is that?"

He explained that not all churches grew in size as the Lord adds to their numbers. Sometimes someone must go out and start a new one.

I wasn't sure I wanted to do that; I liked it where I was. I'd never been happier in my life. Why would I want to leave?

"Gus, you have to get out here," he told me. When I asked him why, he explained, "Because I'm leaving. I'm going back to Texas. You can't believe how much I protect you. Everything you do is irritating to the deacons."

I couldn't believe it! "But all we have is growth in character and numbers to the glory of God!"

"Yeah," he agreed, "but you had a concert here." We'd had a college concert, and everyone loved it. The deacons loved Becky's singing and guitar playing and therefore bought her tapes. But when they played her tapes, there was a drum in the background and the deacons were furious. Someone was playing…the *drums!* (Awful, I know, but this was the era we were in.) "Now they want you out of here," he explained.

"Because someone was playing the drums?"

I was stunned. Pastor Tom went on, "I understand, it's ridiculous." Then he went on, "I think you should go to Hawaii. That's where you were raised, right?"

"Right," I answered. "Where's the hardest place to minister in Hawaii?" I asked. Because of course, that's where I would want to go! Where's the glory for God when it's easy?

And that was that—we were leaving our church in Phoenix for the great unknown to plant a church in Hilo, Hawaii.

About three months later we moved to Hilo. Hilo is a town on the Big Island. I had no idea how hard things would be. Hilo was one of the last stands for local Hawaiian people and therefore a little bit prejudice towards white people. Being raised in Hawaii through elementary and middle school, I understood it. But we rented a school building and started. It was hard, and we ended up only being there for about ten months when our church in Phoenix, which was supporting the church plant, told us they would no longer be supporting us financially anymore. The phone call went something like this: "We want to let you know as of this day we will no longer be supporting you financially. You will no longer receive any checks as of this day. May our Lord bless you." Then they hung up.

That left us in Hilo, Hawaii, with no income. We had sold our house in Phoenix and used all the revenue from the sale to move and start the ministry, so we had no money and no more coming in. However, we were used to trusting God, and this time was no different.

We started off by finding out what it would take to get back to the mainland. Faith and ignorance are not the same things, so it's okay to get all the facts. However, we knew not to let the facts get bigger than God.

We learned it would cost two thousand dollars to get our furniture, our car, and ourselves back to the mainland. We decided to involve the kids in our prayers. Scotty was twelve, Sandy was ten, and Danny was seven. We invited them to pray with us so they could see the faithfulness of God.

We knelt as a family and prayed, thanking God for who He is, and we thanked Him for sending us to Hawaii and for whatever work He'd done while we were there. "We thank You in advance for all the provisions You have for us. In Jesus' name, we pray, Amen," we finished.

No sooner did we say "Amen," than the phone rang. I picked it up; it was my grandma, calling from Oahu. My grandfather had passed a year earlier, and my grandma and I had a strained relationship for some reason. She had been very critical and seemed to always be upset on how close my grandpa and I were.

"Gus, how are you doing?" she asked.

"I'm good, Grandma, really good," I told her.

She said, "Your Aunt Pat and I just found an account that we didn't know your grandpa had. It has $2,200 in it. Would it be okay if we sent it to you?"

God is so good! He's so beautiful! This was the same day we had learned that we needed two thousand dollars to get home, and we had just finished praying and thanking God for provision! We praised God for the extra two hundred dollars and the amazing answer to prayer.

The irony was that it cost two hundred dollars more than we were told to get our car back, so the $2,200 was *exactly* what we needed to get home! God knew what we needed, and He provided—and we got to show our kids how the Lord answers prayers.

God does answer prayers, but that does not mean that He always simply solves our problems for us. We can often go through tough times and wonder why He's letting us experience such trouble, and when we do, it's natural to wonder why He seems to save us at some times and let us struggle at others. However, that doesn't mean He will answer our "why" question—in fact, He often doesn't tell us why. I have discovered that in every case our faith in Him is what is meant to grow and live. Hebrews 11:6 tells us that *"without faith it is impossible to please God, because anyone who comes to him must believe that he exists and that he rewards those who earnestly seek him"* (NIV). He will always be with us, even when things are tough...which they were about to be for us.

We moved back to Phoenix, but we did not go back to the old church. Instead, we started a church in our home while I went back to roofing. It was during this time that many compounding factors began to catch up to Karen.

In hindsight, she can see that her depression and feelings of sadness had returned. She was deeply exhausted, emotionally and physically, and she had many demands on her. With me roofing by day and ministering on weekends and many evenings, Karen handled much of the parenting. In addition to hosting the church in our house, we also had a guy who lived with us for a while, so we had little privacy. Other churchy activities went on during the week, so we were always busy.

While I was growing deeper in love with the Lord and my wife, Karen was struggling with her relationship with Him. You may remember that when we were newly married, I would hypocritically point out her every action that wasn't godly. That and other doubts had stewed behind the scenes together with the depression, feelings of inadequacy, exhaustion, and stress. When she looked at me spending so much time with God and chasing so hard after Him, she compared her own experiences and the fact that she is simply wired differently than I am.

The result: She felt there was something wrong with her. She felt like she wasn't good enough. She felt like I was good, and she judged herself as pretty bad. After nine years of marriage, Karen continued to tell me that I shouldn't have married her.

Some other Christians were critical of Karen's past—that she'd been married and then got divorced—and while she was brave to share her testimony, some people told her that she shouldn't be in the ministry because of that. Those statements lodged in Karen's heart and were doing real damage. It especially impacted her ability to be in groups of Christian women.

It all seemed to come to a head when our houseguest, Al, walked into the bathroom while Karen was in there. The feeling of not having any privacy, even in her own home, caused a chain reaction with all the other feelings that had been piling up, and she felt like she was just coming undone.

Right at that time, Karen's parents came to visit in their motorhome. They asked if they could take our youngest two kids, Sandy and Danny, with them on vacation in the motorhome—Scott often came roofing with me quite a bit. Without thinking it through, Karen wanted to go with her parents. She found she was desperate for a break, to just get out. Once in the motorhome, leaving all the difficulties and strains of life behind, she suddenly felt like she could breathe again.

She later explained that her decision to get away for a vacation in the motorhome with her parents evolved into something else—she didn't want to go back to that. She explained that it wasn't even not coming back to me; it was going back to that life, period. Once gone away from the home, the church, the houseguest, the constant demands of ministry, and all the rest...she found she didn't want to return.

She had needed help for some time, but she felt like there was no one to whom she could turn. So, all the doubts, depression, and insecurity stewed until opportunity presented itself.

Karen now shares that she was not making good decisions then—that she was acting selfishly and wasn't very nice. When Scott and I rode my motorcycle up to Provo, Utah, to see her, it was a shocking conversation that did not go well, and it left me stunned and struggling to figure out how to handle my emotions, as well as Scotty's. He heard things he shouldn't have had to hear.

Our family was hanging in the balance, teetering on the brink of falling apart. It looked grim, and I had no way of knowing what would happen. Would God come through and save my marriage? Would we get divorced, and He'd use that somehow? I just didn't know.

All I knew was that my wife was hurting and running—from me and the life we'd built together. She was depressed, battling extreme feelings of inadequacy, and struggling in her faith.

I was so focused on all the details of ministry and work, I had failed to see how much trouble she was in. With my own walk with our Lord so close, I somehow never saw how undone Karen had become.

You may be facing a tough situation right now. You may have prayed about it, cried about it, anguished over it, and begged God to change it…and yet not see any change. This can be a confusing experience because we're told to trust God to save us.

Sometimes we pray, and mountains move—immediately! Like the phone call we received from my grandmother that paid to get us home from Hawaii, we all love those times. We pray, God answers—boom! Sometimes checks come in the mail from unexpected sources, sometimes people get healed instantly, and sometimes exactly what we pray for happens just the way we'd hoped it would.

Other times…it doesn't. The money didn't come when we expected. Or we pray and pray but see no improvement in a health problem. Or we don't receive the answer we want from God in the way we wanted it. It takes a lot of faith and trust in God to survive these situations, and they can be very, very discouraging. Karen leaving was the worst thing that had ever happened to me, and it shook me to my very core. Whatever dark place you may be in right now, know that you are not alone—many others have felt the same way or have experienced their own version of that hell.

In the years since, I have learned a few things that may help—not help get what you want, but help you navigate these troubling waters—and I want to share with you some highlights.

The foundation is remembering that God is with you, and He isn't going anywhere. Hebrews 13:5 says, *"Let your conduct be without covetousness; be content with such things as you have. For He Himself has said, 'I will never leave you nor forsake you.'"* Even when we do not get what we want, we strive to live in contentment with God. This doesn't mean we don't hope and dream; it means that we find our satisfaction in *His Person*, not the things we want Him to do for us.

Remember also that God is a loving Father, and He cares deeply when His kids struggle and suffer. Psalms says He catches our tears in a bottle, and He is close to the brokenhearted. *"You keep track of all my sorrows. You have collected all my tears in your bottle. You have recorded each one in your book"* (Psalm 56:8 NLT). *"The LORD is close to the broken-hearted; he rescues those whose spirits are crushed"* (Psalm 34:18 NLT).

A perfect picture of how much God cares is found in Jesus coming to raise Lazarus from the dead in John 11, which I encourage you to read in its entirety the moment you're done with this chapter. The world needed to see that Jesus was Lord even over death, and so Jesus let Lazarus die instead of just healing him. When He arrives, Mary and Martha are discouraged, struggling, even doubting. Why, they wonder, couldn't Jesus have saved this one He loved?

Jesus doesn't berate them for asking where He's been—instead, *He grieves with them.* I don't think Jesus was mourning Lazarus' death as we would because Jesus knew He was going to raise Lazarus from the dead.

Instead, I believe He cried because it saddened Him that people He loved were experiencing great pain.

God grieves when we suffer, and He inclines His ear to our pleas for help. But sometimes something must die so it can be raised up. Sometimes a simple healing isn't enough—we need a *resurrection*.

Later in John, we read that many people came to believe in Jesus because they heard about Lazarus rising from the dead. His resurrection did what his healing could not do—after all, Jesus healed plenty of people. Many of the Jews were apparently blind and deaf to the miraculous signs Jesus did by healing countless people. However, by raising Lazarus from the dead, Jesus proved He was God's Son, the Messiah, in a way that drew many to Him.

What dying thing in your life needs a resurrection right now? If you knew God as the One who restores people from the dead, could you let it "die," trusting in your heart that He could bring new life to your situation?

Abraham faced this question when God told him to sacrifice his son Isaac on an altar. In fact, it comes to the point that Abraham has his knife raised above Isaac, poised to kill his son on the altar as a sacrifice to God, when the Lord calls him off at the last second.

Why could Abraham do such a thing? Hebrews 11:17-19 tells us that when tested, he was willing to sacrifice his only son, the son of promise through whom God was going to make him the father of many nations, because Abraham reasoned that God could raise Isaac from the dead. And, in a way, he did receive his son back from death!

Hard times test our faith. Under the heat of the refining fire, God melts it down to sift out the impurities. Paul puts the trying times in life into this perspective:

"We can rejoice, too, when we run into problems and trials, for we know that they help us develop endurance. And endurance develops

strength of character, and character strengthens our confident hope of salvation. And this hope will not lead to disappointment. For we know how dearly God loves us, because he has given us the Holy Spirit to fill our hearts with his love" (Romans 5:3-5 NLT).

God loves you very dearly, my friend, and troubles in life are not an indicator He has left you, or you're no longer in His will. But He will use the opportunity that troubles present to develop endurance, character, and hope in you. That is why James tells us to consider it an opportunity for great joy when we run into troubles, because when troubles test our faith, we have a chance to grow (see James 1:2-4).

So, if you're in a troubling time right now, just tell yourself, "Growth spurt!" Don't lose hope. God cares deeply, and He is with you. He is the God of the living, not the dead, and He is in the resurrection business.

CHAPTER 18:

FIRSTHAND RESTORATION

If you put any of us in the wrong situation long enough and then give us a chance to get out, most of us will eventually take it. If we're not getting help and restoration along the way, we can all reach our breaking point. That's what happened to Karen—she was in a difficult situation for an extended period of time, and when an avenue of escape presented itself, she took it. A vacation away with her folks, however, turned into far more, and it broke my heart, as well as Scotty's, our oldest son.

Scotty and I rode back to Phoenix after visiting Karen in Provo, Utah, crying the whole six-hundred-mile journey. The days that followed were tough for both of us. I was so sick in my stomach over all of this; I lost thirty pounds in the following weeks. For Scotty, it was summer vacation from school, but his sorrow overwhelmed him and he didn't want to do anything. We were both broken and depressed, and nothing I'd learned so far in life prepared me for this.

Scott and I prayed that God would bless Karen and that He would show her He loved her unconditionally. We prayed that she would fall back in love with the Lord. She had forgotten who she was, and we prayed that God would remind her who she was *in Him*.

I started getting counseling at a Christian counseling center in Phoenix, and after all the tests they did, they came back and said they'd never met anyone like me, and somehow their tests showed I was after the heart of God and loved my wife. That information did not help me at all. Time went on, with Karen living in California and me with eventually all three kids in Arizona. We moved from the house we had been renting into an apartment, and I could get back to work roofing. What was so hard was that everyone I knew just seemed to walk away from us. My closest friend in the Lord at the time and a leader in our church plant met with me at a coffee shop to tell me my life and Karen's choices were so bad that he never wanted to see me again. Then he got up and left. He was true to his word; I never saw or heard from him again. It was me and our three kids and our Lord. Oh, of course I left the ministry and handed the church plant over to a new pastor.

About four months after Karen left, I went to answer a knock at the door. I'd finally come to terms that my marriage was likely over and was trying to move on emotionally as well as provide the kids a sense of normalcy.

But who was at the door? Karen! "What are you doing here?" I asked her, not unkindly, just surprised.

"I want to come home!"

She was there in time for Danny's birthday, and over the next couple of days she was there, we talked about our marriage, our family, and our life together. She had driven over to Phoenix in her mom and dad's van, so we talked about how and when to get that back to them. She was also working in California and wanted to go back and give notice. So, she went back to California, and two weeks later I went out to pick her up.

She later told me that God had gotten her attention. All through her attempt to escape, she never felt like He left her. He was always with her. However, one day as she was sitting by herself, talking to the

Lord, she felt this overwhelming sense of, "What are you doing? This is ridiculous; get your act together, and go back to where you belong!" She felt like this was from the Lord, and it was as though He opened her eyes.

She knew it was time to go back and start doing things right. She had missed the kids a bunch and hopefully me, and she knew she wasn't accomplishing anything there trying to live out what she thought "freedom" would be like. Living with her parents, Karen had realized she wasn't happy in the carefree life she'd thought she wanted. She knew she hadn't found the answer. She didn't want to come back to our old life, but she didn't want to stay there in California, either. She just couldn't keep going without her family together.

We needed to make some changes, that was for sure, but she couldn't be part of those changes from California if her family was in Arizona. It was time to go back.

And so she did, and I met her at the front door when she knocked, not having known she was coming.

I won't lie—at first, I was angry with her and closed off. I didn't want her back; I didn't want to go through more hurt if she decided to leave again. I had to live the forgiveness I preached to people, and I had to give the very grace I had received. It was not easy.

However, Karen's visit was a very good time. We quickly let the tension slip from between us to enjoy Danny's birthday, and it was a time for healing to begin.

As I said earlier, Karen had a job in California, and she wanted to go back and give her two weeks' notice, and then the plan was she'd come back to Phoenix. It was very hard to let her leave. I didn't want her to go. I thought if she went back to California and was still seeing her new friends there, she would change her mind again and stay in California.

When I was going to Bible College, I would come back and share everything I learned with Karen, and while I was away at work or school, she would often spend time with the Lord. We were both getting to know Him more deeply, and we were growing together.

However, some interactions with others and books she read gave life to a lie within her—that the Christian life is about performance. And that gave way to a judgment against herself: I can't do this. The focus on performance and perfect background revealed to her all these perceived shortcomings. She felt like she was not a good enough person to do all the things she felt she was supposed to do.

Her relationship with Christ went from an experience of grace to being focused on works—what she could *do* trying to *earn* God's love. This performance focus made her feel there was no way she could do everything required to be a "good Christian woman" or a pastor's wife. It likely didn't help that God called me to certain disciplines, such as my aggressive reading of His Word, which were not activities He'd called her to. She had a different path, but comparison stole her joy and eventually even her confidence in her salvation.

We had both deviated from learning to know God better and were focusing on understanding more about God during a period in our lives, and it planted a terrible seed we would later harvest there in Phoenix.

We can do the "right" things—good things—and still be in the "wrong" because our motives are out of whack.

For Karen, trying to "succeed" at Christianity by performing had seeds that reached at least back to high school. Even in high school, she found herself always comparing herself to others and never feeling good enough or measured up. What she felt was less important, inferior, and not as good as others. Certain strict churches she'd visited in her younger life, where women had to wear dresses and the dress code was important, planted ideas that God's acceptance was based on our performance, not on what He did for us. They made her and others feel judged and conformed to someone's idea of a religious woman.

When she got saved but eventually moved away from knowing God to just learning more about Him and doing work for Him, those same feelings came with her into the new chapter of her life. This only grew worse when judgmental people in some of the churches we attended turned their critical spirits on Karen, judging her for her past marriage.

Karen needed to be free of those judgments—first from the judgments she had made on *herself* and *God* before she could be free of the effects of the words and actions of the critical people around her.

It would take years for Karen to be made new in her thinking and emotions and who she really was because of the grace in Jesus the Christ. Those years were difficult and hard, but in the end those times produced in Karen a beautiful life of grace. She learned for real that *"there is now no condemnation for those who are in Christ Jesus"* (Romans 8:1 NIV).

In the movies, the restoration of a relationship is often where they fade to credits. We see the two, in love once more, embracing, kissing, and all is well. It's a perfect storybook ending, and the audience is free to make up in our minds how wonderful things were for them now they were back together. Surely, it'd be easy from here, right?

For us, it was no storybook. I didn't want Karen to go back to California to give notice and quit her job, and two weeks later when I went to pick her up, we argued the whole way home. Inside, she started to feel like it was a mistake to come back, and I was slow to accept that we needed to make some changes in our lives.

We both had to decide to forgive, and we both had to give one another grace and time to heal the wounds we'd inflicted on one another. But I've loved Karen from the first time I laid eyes on her, and the forgiveness and grace we extended to each other was an opportunity to learn more about the restoration God extends to us as His children. He used our troubles to give us a very personal, up-close lesson in grace.

There's only ever been one perfect Person—and none of us are Him! That is a title only Jesus has ever been able to rightly claim. Likewise, there's never been a perfect marriage. Even in the Garden of Eden, there was dysfunction; from Adam's lack of leadership when the serpent was tempting Eve to the first sibling rivalry ending in murder. If you think your family is bad, just look at the challenges the very first family on earth faced!

As of writing this, Karen and I have now been married 47 years! We have been through a great deal together, from health challenges to car accidents to getting fired to moving halfway across the country (or the world) for opportunities that did not pan out the way we expected. We've ministered together in all kinds of different settings, and we've seen God move in miraculous ways through the two of us together I do not think He could've done had we been apart.

It's been an incredible journey—one that's far from done! Central to the longevity of our marriage is that we have learned to give one another grace and love—the same overwhelming grace and love God has given to us.

When Karen left Phoenix, it was the biggest crisis of our marriage. We were poised on the edge of destruction, but God brought us back from the cliff. What we learned along our journey together is that God's grace brings about a love that forgives well, encourages naturally, and can find a way to give thanks to our Lord in all circumstances. In that place, the joy of the Lord becomes our strength. That is eternal life and not a performance.

We found that even in our tears and heartaches, we could thank our Lord, because those tears and heartaches meant we still loved and that's why we felt the pain. *"Do not be anxious about anything, but in every situation, by prayer and petition,* **with thanksgiving,** *present your requests to God. And the peace of God, which transcends all understanding, will guard your hearts and your minds in Christ Jesus"* (Philippians 4:6-7 NIV, emphasis added).

CHAPTER 19:

KNOWING THE NEED MEETER

Going out to Los Angeles to pick Karen up was one of the happiest days of my life. I drove way over the speed limit, leaving Phoenix at 11:00 at night and arriving in LA at 2:45 in the morning! While Karen and I argued the whole way back, they were issues we needed to talk about.

Things needed to change; I saw that now. In fact, everything was going to change, starting with where we lived. We packed up and moved out of the apartment in Phoenix and headed to Colorado Springs, where a friend in the Air Force had built a chapel in his home for the Air Force cadets. They were very kind to us, and they let us stay there while we recovered from what we'd been through and began putting the pieces of our lives back together.

I started roofing in Colorado Springs, but it was January and colder than cold. I was brushing snow off the roof so I could put the material on. I was working, but it wasn't going well, and the people who owned the place we stayed were very gracious to us and bathed us in kindness. We just couldn't get our feet underneath us again, so when Bill Garman called me and offered me my job back with the dairy, we decided to take it even though I didn't want to move back to California. We rented a house in Simi Valley, I worked for the dairy, and the kids went back to school. Most of all, Karen was happy, and we weren't trying to do anything in the ministry. In fact, we didn't even go to church for a time.

We laughed a lot and just enjoyed being with one another, but Karen wasn't ready to really talk about what had happened. I didn't want to bring it up, but every now and then we had to. Mostly, we just left it all alone.

Eventually, we started going to church on Sundays at Allan's old church. Bill Garman went to that church, and so we started going there off and on. Allan had left because of the toxic atmosphere. After Allan left, another pastor came to the church for quite a few years, then he left for the same reasons Allan left. After being there a couple of months, they asked if I would teach Wednesday night Bible studies. So, Karen and I talked about it and prayed over it, then she told me that she thought I should do it. But the next thing you know, the church was growing. The problem was, I didn't want it to grow!

The church had no pastor because it was in a state of turmoil, and before long they asked me to speak on a couple of Sunday mornings. I had no knowledge of the details why Allan or the other pastor had left at that point, but the in-fighting within the church had gotten so bad that they simply couldn't handle it anymore. We had left the church when we were much younger, so we hadn't seen all the strife and trouble that had torn it apart. However, it didn't take long for us to figure out that there were major problems in the church, and while many of the dear people had left, many of the nasty ones had stayed. New people coming in produced nothing but complaints from those who had stayed, and eventually the head deacon (Bill Garman) resigned. I realized that I couldn't put my family through the strife and backbiting in that church, so we also left with Bill and his family.

We began attending a new church in a denomination we'd never been in before, (Grace Brethren) and we liked the preacher, John Gillis. He was pretty good! At the end of the service, he wanted to meet me, but I didn't really want to talk to him—we just wanted to remain anonymous. We took off! In fact, we didn't go back for a few weeks, and when we did, we wanted just to sneak in and then get away without talking to anyone.

It wasn't to be. The next time we went to that church, the pastor made a beeline for us after the service. "Gus," he said, "come here and meet this guy. Harold, this is Gus."

Harold was my cousin! I reached out and hugged him, and we rejoiced together because we hadn't seen each other in years. That put a confused look on John Gillis' face. Harold said to John, "Gus is my cousin!" Then he said, "Did you know Gus is a preacher?"

The cat was out of the bag.

Seemingly no sooner than my cousin told him that, the pastor turned to me and asked, "Gus, would you preach for me next Sunday?"

"You've never heard me preach," I countered. "What if I'm a weirdo?"

The pastor just smiled. "I'm sure you're not—you're Harold's cousin."

I agreed to do it. That next Sunday, I preached. I didn't even want to do an invitation, but they asked me to. I didn't have a watch, we were so broke, so I had to borrow one to put on the pulpit so I knew what time it was and there was no clock in the church worship center. I preached, and I grudgingly gave this invitation: "If you'd like to receive this life in Jesus the Christ that is eternal and will change your life forever, then come. If not, stay seated on your butts."

And a great multitude got up and came forward! There was standing room only. Except instead of being glad, I just wanted to get out of there. God was ready to move, but apparently, I wasn't.

The pastor was so impressed by the reports he received; he asked me if I'd like to work together with him. I wasn't sure I wanted to get back in the ministry—I wasn't certain that we were ready. Karen had to want to do this, so I asked her what she thought about it.

"I think we should do it," she confirmed. That was enough for me. We were back in the ministry.

Things were a little different at Grace. I had to get rebaptized—three times forward, in fact, for the Father, the Son, and the Holy Spirit, but it was just my head dipping forward. I'd only been baptized backward, so apparently this was important.

Another interesting thing was that the leaders had to wash each other's feet every time we served communion. I didn't like this part too much in the beginning; I was fine washing others' feet, but it was hard for me to let someone else wash my feet at first.

I didn't know what the pastor wanted me to do, but they hired me on, gave me an office, and asked me to teach the adult Sunday school. They'd never had more than fifty people attend it. I told them I would be glad to teach God's Word, but I could not guarantee that the class would grow. But just a few months after I started teaching that class, we had over two hundred people every week!

Immediately, there was tension between the pastor and me. I was really confused over his attitude, and I wondered if I'd offended him, and he began to make things miserable for me, so eventually I told him that I was there to help him and that I'd help by doing this—resigning. He felt jealous, and I didn't want to stay there and cause contention, so we left.

Twelve years later, John Gillis had started a church in Alaska, and we had started a church in Idaho at the time. A man named Max and his family started attending our church in Post Falls, Idaho. He and his family were from Simi Valley and had gone to Grace Brethren. They were there when we were and became some of our dear friends. He told me that he was in contact with John Gillis and that John had been looking for me for years. Then he asked me if I would be willing to meet with John and him. I said of course I would. I had forgiven John the moment I left the church.

So he contacted John in Alaska, and within a couple of weeks we set up a meeting at a resort on the Spokane River and he was flying down.

I was already in the restaurant when John and Max came in. When we saw each other, I got up and John came running over. We instantly hugged each other, and, in tears, he asked me to forgive him. He then told me that he had been asking God for years to let him find me. We rejoiced well in our Lord together. He went on to say that he had never felt jealousy like that before and then said, "I can't imagine what we could have done in Simi Valley if I hadn't been so sinful." John Gillis is truly a great man of God!

I didn't know it at the time we left Grace, but God had a plan that would work out exceedingly well—for our good. Even when dealing with sinful people exercising their free will—which is all of us!—God is never thrown off stride. He has it well in hand, that while it may not always be easy for us, God is always on the throne and has never once been surprised or out of ideas.

At the time of trials and painful events, we don't know how things are going to work out. It's easy for you to read about the way that story would come around over a decade later, but at the time we had no such knowledge—only the assurance that God is good and that we could trust Him.

Since I had quit the dairy to be on staff at Grace, I now had nothing to do. I asked God what I should be doing. Roofing? Back to the dairy? Driving semitrucks? But I kept hearing that God wanted me to do *nothing*. He would take care of our finances.

A friend of ours gave us her late husband's 1972 750cc Honda motorcycle. It needed a lot of work, so I spent the next three months doing little but taking this bike apart and putting it all back together. When I was done, it was beautiful!

Throughout that whole time, money just came in. We didn't know where it would come from, but God provided somehow—checks in the mail, a stack of money three inches high in our mailbox, which was nearly a thousand dollars, and other random things. We had to trust

God completely, and He met our every need. His Word is always true: *"So do not worry, saying, 'What shall we eat?' or 'What shall we drink?' or 'What shall we wear?' For the pagans run after all these things, and your heavenly Father knows that you need them. But seek first his kingdom and his righteousness, and all these things will be given to you as well"* (Matthew 6:31-33 NIV).

I will tell you this: God is the best employer out there. When you trust Him, not your job, it's so much better than putting your faith in your job or yourself as the provider. I would rather God be taking care of us than anything else because He just does it better.

That doesn't mean it's always easy, and often God is very creative with how He provides. You must set aside your pride and accept that His ways are not like our ways. When we work at a job, we work for the glory of God so that our employer can be blessed through our efforts.

One way He provided for us was through my uncle, who owned some car dealerships. He had come to that Baptist church to hear me preach, and afterward, he told me to see him at the store. He offered me a job—and to make me a millionaire in five years! This was a tempting offer because at the time we didn't have a single vehicle in the family. But while I was honored he'd offer, I couldn't do it. We discussed it, and I told him I'd pray about it.

A week later, I came back with a Bible I'd bought him. I had it engraved with his name on it. I thanked him for the offer, but I told him, "I've been called to something else. I would love to make that kind of money. I've always wanted to be a millionaire, but God has called me to something different, so I can't do it."

Then I gave him the gift, and when he opened it up and saw the Bible, he burst into tears. "Gus," he told me, "no one's ever given me a Bible before."

He knew we didn't have a car and asked me about it. "No, we're having a rocky time right now," I told him.

"Tell you what," he said. "Go downstairs and have my sales manager take your picture. We'll put your card on the wall. If you ever send somebody and they buy something, it will show you as a salesman here. Every two months, I want you to have a brand-new Volvo."

And I did. For two years, I drove ten different Volvos, like I was a car dealer. We had no money, but we had a brand-new Volvo!

Another time, Karen's dad gave us his old Ford camper van. The transmission had gone out, and the inside was all trashed. I took it to the transmission store and asked how much it would cost, and it was $425.00. Well, we didn't have any money, and so as a family, we asked God to provide the money.

Well, about a week later, the guy at the transmission shop called me and told me our van was ready. I went over, thinking maybe I could make payment arrangements, but when I got there he just handed me the keys! "I haven't paid you," I reminded him.

"It's already paid for," he told me. "Someone came in and paid for it."

We never found out who it was.

Together with help from a guy from our church, we recarpeted the inside, put in new chairs, and installed a table in the back. It was beautiful, and our family probably put over 200,000 miles on that big old van.

I tell you these things not to brag about God's favor on us but to encourage you. I won't lie—those times were tough. We had to make difficult choices, and life was not a rosy bed of comforts and conspicuous spending. But neither did we starve or go without a roof over our heads. Even when we had no vehicles, we somehow were able to get where we really needed to go.

Some in the Church have preached poverty—that we're not supposed to have "things" because materialism corrupts and money is the root of all evil and so forth. (It's not—the love of money is the root of all kinds of evil. See 1 Timothy 6:10). They think in abandoning all worldly ties, they draw closer to God.

Some have preached prosperity—they'll know you're a Christian because you drive a Lexus and are wealthy. They think that you should always have conspicuous money, by Western standards, and should impress your nonbelieving friends with your extreme wealth.

The real answer, I think, is that God's provision isn't about money at all. It's about *Himself.*

You've read this repeatedly in this book: The greatest gift God can give us is *Him.* Being a Christian and learning God's promises is not about discovering the right formula or Scripture or belief to twist His arm into giving you what you want.

It's in knowing Him that you learn He is with you, He loves you, and He's got it all figured out because *that's who He is.* That's His character. Our faith and trust are not in what He does for us; they are in He Himself.

With that understanding in mind, read these verses: *"And my God shall supply all your need according to His riches in glory by Christ Jesus"* (Philippians 4:19). And, *"God will generously provide all you need. Then you will always have everything you need and plenty left over to share with others"* (2 Corinthians 9:8 NLT). Notice, both are talking about God providing, but neither directly mentions money.

He is the Need Meeter. He is the Provider. He is our Resource, and our trust is to be in Him and Him alone.

It's about knowing Him, dear reader. No matter what you're going through, He is enough. Whether you need money, or peace, or health, or patience, Jesus the Christ is your answer. Everything else will fall into place when you look to Him first. It's not about what you want Him to do for you; it's about *Him.*

CHAPTER 20:

CHURCH PLANTING

God has an amazing way of providing for us, even when we've messed up. His grace is that good!

We left Grace, though at the time we didn't know that the Lord would bring restoration between the pastor and myself. We went through a period of doing nothing, but then God's plan for us began to reveal itself. We entered a new period of our lives where we no longer were visiting churches and looking to join something someone else was doing, but instead God put it on our hearts to start something new and fresh.

A friend whom we'd led to Christ wanted to start a new church with us, and about four months after our initial conversations, we launched a church in a single-car garage in Simi Valley. It was the first real church we'd started on our own, and we called it Calvary Memorial Church. We would eventually change the name to Calvary Evangelical Free Church.

We cleaned out the garage and moved in a piano, and it could hold about sixteen people, but twenty-three showed up! Some of them had to sit outside. Before we knew it, seventy, eighty, even ninety people were sitting in the driveway, many of them holding umbrellas to provide shade in the bright Southern California sunlight. Someone suggested renting a building, which I hadn't thought of, and we eventually did rent one in an industrial park.

Our Lord overwhelmed us with His grace and presence. I started preaching in Ephesians, and to my amazement individuals and families came. The joy of our Lord was our strength.

It was here during the early days of Calvary Memorial growing that my mom asked me to go up to Washington to see our relatives. I didn't want to go—we were too busy with the new church. She suggested I take Karen and make a vacation out of it, and at first I resisted. However, one morning when I got up I felt the Lord saying, "Go with your mother and wife to Washington." So, I called my mom and told her I would love to go.

It was a fun trip with my mom and wife; we saw all kinds of relatives from her side of the family that I hadn't seen in years. After visiting Karen's sister and husband in Sumas, Washington, we were driving back to Sedro Woolley in Skagit County. As we entered Bellingham, Washington, which was in Whatcom County, I felt the Lord wanted me to pray. I turned to Karen and said, "God wants me to pray for this place. What am I supposed to pray? We don't know anybody here." But the urging from God was strong, so eventually I said, "You close your eyes; I'll keep mine open, since I'm driving."

I prayed a simple prayer and asked God for His blessing and grace and the wonders of His loving compassion for the people of the community. I thanked Him for the thousands of men and women He was going to lead into His presence.

That was it. I then felt a feeling of sweet relief—I was done and didn't have to pray for that again. But the next day when I woke up, I felt inspired to pray the same thing again for Bellingham, and that went on for the next year and a half.

Our church in Simi Valley had grown to about 175 people, but I simply couldn't shake this burden for Bellingham. Eventually, we decided to go back up to see my cousin Colleen and her husband, and we stayed with them on their place, which was ten acres in Ferndale, which is the city next to Bellingham.

While we were there, Colleen asked me, "Would you ever think of coming up here and starting a church?"

"No," I answered reflexively. "I would never consider it." But the next morning, I felt like the Lord told me that I should not have spoken so quickly. So that morning I went to the back of their wooded property, sat on a log, and began reading God's Word and spending the day talking to the Lord. When I came back that evening, I had to tell them, "Well, I shouldn't have said no. I'm not saying I would say yes, but I shouldn't have said no so fast."

Colleen said, "I'm not saying you would...but if you did, would you consider having church in a funeral chapel?"

"A funeral chapel?" I asked in surprise. "Oh yeah, I can see it, the church of the living dead!"

But they talked me into looking at it. The chapel sat about 140 people, and the owner, Nick Jerns, said that he'd rent it for $200.00 a week, which was reasonable.

"But we already have a church meeting here," he told me.

Oh well, that settles it, I thought. I was leaving, but then Nick asked me to come into his office. "How many people are you talking about?" he asked.

"None, zero," I told him. "The church doesn't exist yet." He looked confused. "Besides, didn't you say you already had a church in here?"

"Well, actually they left about three months ago," he told me.

"I just think God may be doing something, and if He does start doing something, the community is going to change."

He asked, "When are you coming?"

"When? I don't know *if* we're coming," I told him.

"Well," he told me, "I think you're supposed to be here."

We exchanged numbers, and we left. It was an odd meeting, but I did have a feeling God was up to something. I just didn't know what it was.

We went so far as to speak with the Evangelical Free Church superintendent over Oregon and Washington to tell him our pasts to see what his opinion might be of two people like us coming to Bellingham, Washington. We were completely honest, because we didn't want any surprises or hidden agendas this time.

Honestly, I expected that he'd reject us, so we were surprised that the superintendent said, "We have never heard anyone like you. We want you up here! When can you get here?"

I didn't know. Were we going to leave California again and move to Washington? That seemed to be the direction God was leading. But it seemed like we'd just started Calvary Evangelical Free Church—it was less than two years old. Now we were leaving?

We prayed about it, and we decided that if we presented it to the church leadership and they blessed us, we'd know it was God's will. So, we told the church what we had experienced in Washington and they gave us their blessing.

We were going to Washington!

We rented a big Ryder truck and loaded it up, and we hitched a trailer behind our camper van. With Karen driving the van and me driving the Ryder with our other car towed behind it, we headed north.

It wasn't an easy drive for Karen. Part way through, she began to feel sick. She abruptly told Sandy, who was fifteen at the time, to hand her something…because she was about to throw up! Sandy got her a bag, and while still driving and pulling the trailer, Karen was sick. She frantically told me over our walkie talkies to pull off at the next rest stop.

It was a difficult trip, but Karen made it to my cousin Colleen's house, where she collapsed because she felt so sick. Colleen had thoughtfully made a big pot of clam chowder—which Karen couldn't even *look at*.

Colleen had been helping us look for a place to live. We basically told her we wanted at least three bedrooms and real-life trees—a rare commodity when you're coming from Southern California. She found us this old farmhouse on the lot of a roofing company. When we got in and got unloaded and Karen could sit upright, we headed over to see it.

It was the leaning Tower of Pisa of farmhouses—old and sagging. "Are you kidding?" I asked Karen. We just exchanged a look. This was our house, at least for now.

We started getting our stuff in. We had a waterbed in those days, and it fit exactly wall-to-wall in the master bedroom, though I had to shim it on one side so it wouldn't overflow on the low side of the house.

Well, the owner came to see us, and he told me he didn't allow dogs. Of course, we had two dogs, Heidi and Hunter, and our cat whose name was Harley Davidson. I thought, "Praise God, we're out of here!" We kept our stuff in boxes and started looking for another place.

However, we couldn't find *anything* anywhere nearby! After three days of looking, the owner suggested we build a dog run by the house. Since we couldn't find anything else, we figured we needed to make the best of it, so we made this beautiful log dog run.

We arrived in Bellingham with $238 to our name. Our whole Christian lives had been this way, however, so we were used to it. I just asked the Lord what I was supposed to do. Karen was still sick, Scotty was eighteen and headed to a college in Canada, Sandy was in high school, and Danny was in the eighth grade. Was I supposed to go into roofing? After all, the house we were in was right next to a roofing company.

I spent three days in the living room praying and asking God for direction.

God, I prayed, *did I make a mistake? I thought You sent me here. Is that true? Or did I hear wrong?*

On the third day, I heard from God. I felt He said, "I sent you here, Gus. Not only did I send you, and not only am I your Father, I am your employer all the days of your life."

I came out of my prayer time and confidently told Karen, "God said He's our employer. Don't worry about it."

Four more days passed, and little seemed to change on the outside, except Karen was feeling better. But inside, I felt at peace. Karen and I were in the kitchen, looking at our nineteen cents (all the money we had left), when we heard a knock at the door.

A good-looking young blond-haired man was there. "Are you Gus Bess?" he asked. I said I was. "The Lord sent me."

"The Lord sent you? I've never heard anyone say that before. Come on in."

"I can't come in," he said, "because I'm just here to give you these envelopes. The Lord's blessings to you," he said, and then he turned around and walked off, having given me two envelopes.

I went back into the kitchen to show Karen. One envelope had the word "Church" written on it. The other said "Gus Bess." We opened them quickly. The envelope marked "Church" contained two thousand dollars! And the other also held another two grand! I was astounded. We had no debt, no car payments or anything, and we now had four grand for ourselves and the church startup. God is so good!

When I went to pay our rent, Hank who owned the house said, "I don't want your money. I'm just glad you're in that house."

"No," I insisted, "I want to pay my rent."

"You're not paying rent," he told me. "You're living there for free." I would discover that Hank was a great man after the heart of God and he became a dear friend.

The handsome young blond guy came every month for four months and gave us two thousand for us and two thousand for the church. I didn't find out who he was for over a year and a half, when I learned what had been happening. All I knew was that God had called us, and He provided the money for us to get started. He was our employer, and He made sure that we had what we needed to do the work He'd called us to do.

What has God called you to do? It doesn't have to be starting a church or a ministry for God to have something important in mind for you. God isn't just interested in pastors and preachers and evangelists; He has assignments for each one of us. They're all important to the Kingdom of God, and He equips and provides for us so that we can do whatever work He has called us to do and enjoy it as we do it.

We can become confused by the lie that God is only really interested in those in full-time ministry. After all, most of the people who tell fantastic God stories are—surprise, surprise—in the ministry! They've gotten checks in the mail, envelopes full of cash, or rent-free houses, and if you have not experienced such a thing, it can leave you wondering if God even cares about the rest of Christianity.

I want to tell you something important: While some people may call the full-time ministry their vocation, we are *all* called to be ministers of the Gospel of Jesus the Christ. Not all of us will be in "the ministry," and that is for the best! God needs you in place, doing His assignments, right where you are—at your job, at your school, or wherever else God may have you. You are His ambassador all the time, no matter where you are employed. You're in His ministry.

God will equip those He calls. He is building you up and equipping you with exactly what you need to do what He calls you to do. But if you have been intimidated or lulled into laziness by thinking God only works through pastors and evangelists, you can take for granted the assignment He has given to you.

When is the last time you stopped and asked God what He wants you to be doing? When is the last time you asked for His vision and will for your life? Because if you are unaware of His calling for you, you will be unaware of the things He miraculously does to equip and provide for you. Blessings and miracles (big and so small you can easily miss them) may come and go in your life, and you can fail to notice because you have discounted the call of God upon your life.

Have you ever thought about buying a certain kind of car and then started to notice that type of car seems to be *everywhere?* Suddenly, you notice them. Before they were on your radar, you likely didn't pay any attention. But now that you're interested, now that you're *looking*, you find them everywhere. God's blessings are like that. If God's purpose is on your radar, when He provides for you, you will notice it. When you're not paying attention, you can go right past them without even seeing them.

In Matthew 7:7-8 Jesus says, *"Ask, and it will be given to you; seek, and you will find; knock, and it will be opened to you. For everyone who asks receives, and he who seeks finds, and to him who knocks it will be opened."* You must *ask.* Ask, and keep on asking; look, and keep on looking. If you do, you will find—God guarantees it in His Word.

"If [your child] *asks for bread, will* [he] *give him a stone? Or if he asks for a fish, will he give him a serpent?"* (vv. 9-10). Of course not. So why do we assume that God would give us bad things? Why would we think that God would call us to something and then leave us hanging, or send

us into a dangerous situation just to see us fail? Jesus goes on to say, "*If you then, being evil, know how to give good gifts to your children, how much more will your Father who is in heaven give good things to those who ask Him!*" (Matthew 7:11).

God is ready to provide for the assignment He has given you. He has placed a calling upon your life, but it's your job to ask Him what it is. In the story in this chapter, we prayed for days. But sometimes it takes weeks, months, or even *years!* Abraham waited for decades for God's promise to be fulfilled. So why would we get discouraged and quit asking after hours or days? Ask Him, and then actively look for His provision for you. It will be there, because He promises that if you ask you will receive and if you seek you will find.

Luke puts a slightly different twist on the Scripture from Matthew I quoted above. He says, "*So if you sinful people know how to give good gifts to your children, how much more will your heavenly Father give the Holy Spirit to those who ask him*" (Luke 11:13 NLT).

God is a giver of good gifts…and the best one is Himself! Are you looking for Him?

CHAPTER 21

FIRST CHURCH OF THE LIVING DEAD

We had funding for the first time I can ever remember—for four months, this handsome blond guy came each month to give us two thousand for the church and another two for us. We had money in our account! It was a strange feeling.

I only later learned the story of what happened there. It turned out that Hank Scholten of Scholten Roofing, a pretty big deal up there, and as I have already said, was a great man of God. He was the man I met that day we arrived, when he told me they didn't have dogs. The blond guy was Galen, and apparently Hank told Galen he thought they should tithe on the company profits every month. Hank told Galen that he thought God was doing something with us and that the Lord was with "that young preacher" (me).

Because of their obedience, God got the church off to a fast start. And because we had no car payments, no housing expenses (remember, we were living rent-free in the old leaning farmhouse), and the utilities were so low, we were able to save up thousands of dollars and fund the church well right from the start. At the end of four months, tithes were coming in through the church, and we had the jump start we needed!

God took care of us from that time on like we were independently wealthy. We almost never had any money, yet when God wanted to do something, the money simply came in to do it to the tune of hundreds of thousands of dollars. Anything the Lord wanted to do, He funded. It was just always there for whatever He instructed, and when we didn't even have a dime in the bank, it was never a barrier to going forward with the Lord's instructions.

About a week and a half after getting the money the Lord sent to help start the church and fund us being there, I was walking through downtown Bellingham when I saw a handsome guy in a suit about my age. He was smiling, so I said hello and struck up a conversation.

"Where are you from?" he asked.

"I'm from California," I told him. "What do you do?"

"I'm an attorney," he answered. "What about you?"

I told him, "I'm here to start something and make a difference. What kind of lawyer are you?"

"I'm a divorce lawyer," he answered. "So, what have you come to do?"

I smiled really big at this. "I'm here to put you out of business," I told him.

That was a start of a friendship, and that man came to Christ about a year later. He also ended up getting married, becoming very wealthy, and helped many marriages to become successful.

And that's just how things happened in Bellingham—we didn't advertise, but we just told people about what we were doing there. And they came!

They told me to start the church in the county, because county folks wouldn't drive into the "city," and city folks wouldn't come to the county (it was a difference of just four miles). Well, we were committed to meeting in Nick Jerns Funeral home, and so right away we had obstacles to overcome—a church located in the "wrong place" and that was meeting in a funeral home! I joked that it was the church for the living dead!

Yet *they came!*

The first Sunday we met was September 16, 1984, and I had no idea if anyone would come. But they did. We knew my cousin Colleen and a few other family members would come, but beyond that, we had not advertised; we'd just spoken to people freely. And that fist week, twenty-seven people showed up. It was fun, but to get ready, we had a little bit different preparation work than many churches.

At our church, we had to move the dead bodies before the living bodies showed up! They didn't do funeral services on Sundays, but they had people's loved ones arranged in the foyer and other areas for viewings.

Fittingly, there was an organ, and my cousin Colleen could play the piano and organ. I had to stand just in a certain place so she could see me to get her cues of when to start or stop playing. We had a blast! It was very exciting because we were doing what God had called us to do, and people came—into the city, to a funeral home full of dead bodies, to come to the Evangelical Free Church of Bellingham!

Though that first week was a success, I determined it would be better if the bodies weren't in the foyer to greet people, so I asked if I could come in Saturday night and move the bodies out for services. Nick Jerns, the owner, said I could, if I moved them back again. So, I started coming in on Saturdays and moving three, four, even five bodies from the foyer into some of the other rooms. I even used the little room the florist used, which was behind some curtains where I stood and preached. I did not think anything about it because no one would know anyone was there behind the curtain. At times, I even moved them back into the cooler.

Well, one morning, perhaps in our third week, around 9:00 a.m. a car pulled into the parking lot. A woman got out of the car, and she was crying. I knew she wasn't here for church.

I was wearing my suit—I always dressed in a suit in those days—and so I tried to be sensitive as I greeted her. Tears poured down her face as she said, "I am here to see Bob."

"You're here to see Bob?" I echoed. Uh-oh. I'd moved all the bodies around, and I had no idea which one was Bob. I had not expected to have any viewings before church, so because there were so many that weekend, I had stuffed them in any room I could quite haphazardly! That morning I had put someone in the florist closet behind the curtain, I couldn't even shut the door; I'd just pulled this curtain so no one could see the door was cracked open and a dead body was right in there.

I said, "Ma'am, I'm afraid I'm not quite sure where Bob is now. I will need to show you a few of them." I was praying he wasn't one in the overflowing closet with the open door!

I showed her the first body. "Is this Bob?" I asked.

She shook her head, crying, and managed to say, "No, that's not him."

As I walked to the next body in the next room, I was desperately praying, "Father, please let this next guy be Bob!"

I showed her the body, and her tears started flowing even harder. We had found Bob! I was so grateful I didn't need to show her the closet.

The church just grew and grew. The chapel held 144 people, but we also had kids (which Karen handled nearly by herself for the longest time). The back of the chapel was glass, so eventually when we just couldn't pack them in any tighter, we pulled the curtains to the foyer and people could stand and *watch* the service from the foyer. It was certainly an incentive to get to church on time!

The last year and a half we were in the funeral home, we got up to 320 people in the building for our morning and evening services. First time guests and seniors got to sit in the 144 seats; everyone else had to stand. Yet they still came! One creative guy even turned a construction trailer into a nursery, which was great because funeral homes do not have a lot of sound deadening material in the walls. After all, the typical occupants aren't very noisy—they're dead!

After this experience in Bellingham, people started asking me to teach them how to plant churches, but I had to tell them that it wasn't anything we planned. God builds His own Church, which He did with us, and we were just along for the ride. I told them that it is our job to chase after God in a way that others cannot help but notice so that they will follow us to Him. We want others to know God the way we know Him.

The perfect situation is not being a gifted leader, teacher, pastor, worship leader, or anything else—it's knowing God. It has always been my dream that people would see the Jesus on me and in me, and that is what would attract them to me and from there point toward the Father.

In all honesty, I can confidently say that *hundreds* of people have told me, "I want to know the Jesus you know." It is the highest form of praise, and it is what I want to hear when I stand before our Lord—that I pointed the way to the Father.

We experienced explosive church growth, but it was nothing for which I can take credit. I am not so great an apostle, teacher, or leader that by myself I could generate that kind of reaction: I was just a reflection of Jesus.

This is a key position or attitude—one of humility. If you begin to think it's *you*, that you're the reason the people are coming, or God is doing things, or make it about yourself in any way, you're getting into pride. It is never about us; it's always about Him.

Jesus walked this out. Listen to how He answered people: *"Most assuredly, I say to you, the Son can do nothing of Himself, but what He sees the Father do; for whatever He does, the Son also does in like manner. For the Father loves the Son, and shows Him all things that He Himself does; and He will show Him greater works than these, that you may marvel"* (John 5:19-20).

This echoes the work of the Holy Spirit. Jesus later says, *"However, when He, the Spirit of truth, has come, He will guide you into all truth; for He will not speak on His own authority, but whatever He hears He will speak; and He will tell you things to come"* (John 16:13).

If Jesus, the very Son of God, did not point to Himself and could do nothing by Himself, and the Holy Spirit does nothing on His own authority, how important should it be that we never do anything apart from what God says? Knowing God should be our first and overriding passion. Nothing matters without this. Spiritual gifts like healing and prophecy and words of knowledge are nothing if they are not accurately pointing to God first. If we are trying to soak up some of the glory, if we're letting anything point to us instead of to Him, we are out of proper alignment.

Have you ever looked up at the moon at night when it is particularly bright? On nights with a full moon, it can be bright enough to do things outside you might ordinarily only do during the day. But has it ever occurred to you that the moon has no light of its own? The moon does not generate one candle's worth of light itself; it only reflects the light of the sun.

We are to be like the moon to a dark and dying world: reflecting the light and love of God to those who live in darkness. Apart from Him, we can do nothing (see John 15:5). But when we simply reflect Him to others, we shine brightly and bear much fruit.

Then people will say, "I want to know the Jesus you know."

CHAPTER 22:

So You Want to Know the Lord

You may remember from earlier in the book that when I went to seminary, I learned a lot *about* the Lord. However, I didn't want to know more *about* God, I wanted to *know God better*. They are not the same thing, as I learned.

This has been one of the great dilemmas in the Church: How do you help others get to know or want to know the Lord better? It is not through more academics, though studying what He has said about Himself is one way we get to know Him. Pastors and other leaders cannot know God *for* someone, though we can show the way. People must want to know the Lord for themselves. So how do we help them?

In the Word of God, the answer is discipleship. So what is that?

When Jesus began His earthly ministry, He selected twelve people from among all His followers, and He poured into them by spending three years together in close fellowship. These were the ones who got to know Him personally, and in knowing Him, they got to know the Father.

There in Bellingham I was aggressive about discipleship. If people wanted to know the Lord—really know the Lord!—I had two groups they could pick from, one on Monday, and another on Wednesday. For two hours on those evenings, I helped people get to know the Lord.

I loved seeing people who'd just received God's grace in Jesus begin to get to know Him. We talked about the Lord and experienced Him, but they also did two hours of homework every week, including memorizing a Scripture verse each week.

"But I can't memorize Bible verses," some would say.

"What's your phone number?" I asked them. They'd rattle it off, and I would say, "See, you can memorize just fine. When we're done, you're going to know fifty-two different verses of Scripture." I asked them for a one-year commitment, and then I taught them how to get to know God through reading His Word, through prayer, and time together in worship and praise.

"I'll pour everything I have into you," I told them. "This is God's Eternal Breath, and if you shake my hand and agree, you can't quit. If you don't come, you give me permission to come to your house, grab you by the scruff of the neck, and drag you here. And I promise I will!"

People shook my hand right and left—we consistently had twelve or fourteen different people each night. They were hungry for God. They wanted to know Him, and they were willing to invest themselves in the intensive discipleship I offered.

Only one time did I ever come close to dragging someone out of their door. Walt and Bobbie were salt of the earth people—rough around the edges, but good. He was an old fisherman, and we hunted and fished together, becoming good friends. They came to the discipleship class, and they both shook my hand, but six or seven weeks in, Walt showed up alone for class.

"Where's Bobbie?" I asked.

"She's quitting," Walt said. He got this stupid grin on his face and added, "I reminded her that you said you'd come grab her by the neck and drag her out of the house."

I said, "Walt, take over the group. I'm going to your house."

Their place was about five miles away, and I drove over there quickly and knocked on the door. Bobbie answered the door, and I said, "Well, are you coming, or am I going to have to grab you by the neck?"

She said, "Let me go get my Bible."

I saw amazing changes in lives because of that group. Hurting, wounded people who seemed to believe all the right things about the Lord began to change when all they "knew" had not helped them through their stuff. I witnessed our Lord revolutionize things within them, changing the whole landscape of their relationship to Him. You see, when you come to know God through close contact, *He changes things* within you. It's inevitable: connection with God creates life change.

One woman's story stands out in particular. Courtney and Sharon are a wonderful couple, and they are our friends to this day. She's a beautiful woman, but when we met her, she had this strange crease down the middle of her forehead. It was deep, and it looked like it had been etched there permanently like a fold in the terrain of the earth.

We learned she had experienced a grave emotional wound from long ago, and it seems to have come to rest obviously on her face—she bore the physical mark of her pain. When their firstborn was about five, he was playing in the yard with their dog. The dog was on a chain, and somehow the chain became wrapped around the little boy's neck. When the dog suddenly took off running, the chain snapped tight around his neck and killed him. She saw it from the kitchen window.

As though that wasn't traumatic enough, the church they attended treated the news by saying, "Sharon, you need to confess your sin right now! God's already punished you, so we all know you're a sinner!"

There did not seem to be any ministry to the hurt in her soul, no caring and loving her through this horrible time. Those who were to represent God to her instead helped imprint her face with this mark of sadness and anguish by voicing accusations. By the time we met her, she'd lived with that loss for thirteen years. She was this quiet, withdrawn, beautiful woman, and I literally had to force her to talk during the discipleship group.

On her sixth week, Sharon had to write out her testimony and share it. When it came time for her to share, she revealed to us the story of the loss of her son. In that room, surrounded by those who cared for her, the love of God poured out on her. Everyone shared His love with her, and I watched as that crease on her forehead literally vanished before my eyes!

And it never came back.

Sharon was transformed by God's love. Her physical appearance changed, and she became freer and more open to speak and share. For six weeks of discipleship, she had been getting to know who the Lord really is—not the One who kills our children because of some unconfessed sin, but a loving Father who wants to heal our wounds. The grace of God became a reality for her, and she experienced how much God loved her there in the context of community and discipleship.

She needed to know that He loved her no matter what, because she had come to question it. I shared with her that once you've been adopted, you're adopted for life. I told her how I adopted two of my children and that the judge was very clear that I could never unadopt them. God had adopted her, and she had a new nature, and I told her that *"there is therefore now no condemnation for those who are in Christ..."* (Romans 8:1).

We must come to really know that there is no one like our Lord. There are a couple of verses that I believe describe true discipleship well.

"As the deer pants for streams of water, so my soul pants for you, my God. My soul thirsts for God, for the living God..." (Psalm 42:1-2 NIV).

Another is, *"Shout for joy to the LORD, all the earth. Worship the LORD with gladness; come before him with joyful songs. Know that the LORD is God. It is he who made us, and we are his; we are his people, the sheep of his pasture. Enter his gates with thanksgiving and his courts with praise; give thanks to him and praise his name. For the LORD is good and his love endures forever; his faithfulness continues through all generations"* (Psalm 100:1-5 NIV).

Sharon, that precious woman with the crease in her forehead after the loss of her son, needed to know God's heart. She didn't need to know *about Him*, she needed to *know Him*. She needed to experience His love for her, and she did that through discipleship—one person teaching another how to know God and then doing life together with her.

For her, and perhaps for you, this was the life-giving Scripture she needed to not just read but breathe in: *"Therefore, there is now no condemnation to those who are in Christ Jesus... who do not live according to the flesh but according to the Spirit"* (Romans 8:1,4 NIV).

Paul goes on to say, *"For all who are led by the Spirit of God are children of God. So you have not received a spirit that makes you fearful slaves. Instead, you received God's Spirit when he adopted you as his own children. Now we call him, 'Abba, Father'"* (Romans 8:14-15 NLT).

Without knowing God, these are just nice words. They don't resonate in our heart without His presence to inspire them. But when the Spirit that has adopted us sings in harmony with our own spirit made new, these words become the living Breath of God for us.

That is what happened to Sharon—the living Breath of God became alive in her. And that's my desire for you, too. I pray that your desire to know God inspires you to dive in and drink deeply of Him. I pray that His living Word takes up residence *within* you, and that you *know Him.*

That is why it is so important to put His Word in your heart. It cannot resonate within you if it's not *in you*. You've got to put it in. It is not an act of works or the law to read the Bible; you are not just learning "about" God when you read His Word. You're putting within yourself His very breath, His very own words to *you*. When you're alive in Christ, those words come alive in you, and they are powerful! Hebrews tells us, "*For the word of God is alive and powerful. It is sharper than the sharpest two-edged sword, cutting between soul and spirit, between joint and marrow. It exposes our innermost thoughts and desires*" (Hebrews 4:12 NLT).

Paul adds a summary of how vital the Word is by saying, "*All Scripture is God-breathed and is useful for teaching, rebuking, correcting and training in righteousness, so that the man* [or woman] *of God may be thoroughly equipped for every good work*" (2 Timothy 3:16-17 NIV 1984).

I cannot say it too many times. You want God's Breath to become your breath and God's Word to become your word. When this is who we are, those creases and ruts in our life from sin are removed forever!

CHAPTER 23:

A DRAW TO HOLINESS

The church continued to grow. God was doing amazing things, and people just kept coming. I raised my own rent at the funeral home, because I knew that with all the extra traffic was more wear and tear on the facilities. Every six months or so, I gave the owner more money, until by the time we left we were paying $1000 a month. We also cared for our leaning old farmhouse during the time we were there in a way no renter apparently ever had before. I landscaped, kept the yard mowed immaculately, and we treated it with great honor. (This is despite the fact it was infested with spiders so thickly that their webs literally held up a broom! I sprayed them and removed these extra "guests" from our home.)

I believe strongly in treating what you do have with honor, for the glory of God and trusting God to add more to you as you show your faithfulness. We showed ourselves faithful with little, and God blessed us with more.

Eventually, a man of God I met who was a builder offered to rent out some office space to us for a very reasonable amount. He built a very large bookshelf for us to separate this one, large open space into two offices for me and the associate pastor who joined us, Dan.

I have never offered something to God that didn't cost me something. David modeled this principle when he bought the threshing floor and oxen of Araunah, refusing to give God a sacrifice that hadn't cost him something (see 2 Samuel 24:24). That is why I kept raising our rent at the funeral home, and that's why though I got up around 5:30 or 6:00 during the week, on Tuesdays I got up at 4:30 to meet with the Lord.

When we got this office, I thought I should be there at the office, dressed, shaved, and ready for the day, at 4:30. I was doing that, and I don't remember ever telling anyone about it. But one Tuesday when I got to the office at 4:30 in the morning to find there were ten men from the church standing there!

"What are you doing here?" "We've come to pray with you," one said.

I told them bluntly, "I don't want you praying with me; this is my time with the Lord."

"Well," they replied, "we're going to pray with you whether you like it or not."

A prayer meeting started that day that eventually grew to number one hundred men and women! We changed the time to 6 a.m. and got together on Tuesday mornings to seek God together.

We eventually called it a "Battering Ram Against the Gates of Hell," and the only rule was that there was no praying for physical things—it was all spiritual. We did not pray for healing, or finances, or anything else tied to this world. We prayed for people's souls. We prayed for God's Kingdom to come. We prayed for His will for our community, our church, and our families. We prayed for holiness, that set-apart aspect God's people are to have that distinguishes us from this sinful world.

And God answered.

I started something else no one else had done while I was there at Bellingham: I got tired of people saying the sinner's prayer and giving an invitation at Sunday services. Many did this, but it seemed that although they said the prayer, their lives did not change one bit. Instead, I said that people could only be saved on Mondays and Tuesdays, after preaching on Sunday, I would have appointments all day Monday and Tuesday leading people to the Lord. They would beg me in the Sunday service, and I'd ask, "Is it Monday? Is it Tuesday? No? Come then."

I was not a hellfire and brimstone preacher, but people would just be desperate to know God, and they would come. Several of our pastors in the area got really irritated with me and asked things like, "What if these people go to hell?" I would tell them, "That is not my problem. Salvation is not a prayer; salvation is the Lord coming into a man or woman and they become a new creation. All this is from God," and remind them of 2 Corinthians 5:17-18. On those Mondays and Tuesdays when they asked to receive God's grace in Jesus the Christ, they meant it. This went on for almost a year!

Many people began life-changing relationships with Christ this way, but one man in particular had a miraculous story. He wanted to meet with me, and he showed up on a Monday, which surprised me. I asked him, "What are you doing here today?" He told me his story—that he was a helicopter pilot from Canada and so forth. "But, Gus, I have a problem," he told me.

"What's your problem?"

"I'm a homosexual," he told me.

I answered, "Wow."

He went on, "Well, it's worse."

I said, "It's worse?"

He went on to say, "I have…molested boys. That's why I'm down here instead of Canada; they'll catch me if I go back."

I said, "You really need to know our Savior."

He said. "I want to know the Jesus you know!"

We knelt to pray at our chairs, and he wailed so hard, he left a big wet spot in my chair from all his tears! He sounded like he was going to throw up his stomach, he cried so hard. But when he got up, there was a change about him.

He was *different*. He had this indescribable, unspeakable joy inside of him that comes only from the presence of Jesus. I told him I'd meet with him every day, which we did for three weeks. I showed him who he was as a man of God. God's Word showed him that all the old things had passed away and that he'd become new.

We dove deeply into intense discipleship, and at the end of that time, I told him, "You've made it right with God. Now let's go make it right with man."

He said, "Okay."

I told him. "You're going to jail."

He replied, "Let's do it."

I drove him up to Canada, and he turned himself in. I went with him into the courtroom before the judge, and I heard this young man plead guilty. The hate in that room was nearly palpable, but he stayed strong. Eventually, the judge asked, "Do you have anything else you want to say before I pronounce your sentence?"

He did. "Your honor, I don't want this to impact your sentencing at all, but I want you to know that I am a brand-new man. I have come to know Jesus Christ. I don't believe in Him; I *know Him*. But the only way you'll know what I said is true is if you watch me the rest of my life."

That man was sentenced to ten years in prison, and he served four of them before being released. He later got married, had three beautiful daughters, and one of his daughters became a missionary to Africa!

The change in him was profound, and it altered all aspects of his life. Knowing Jesus changed everything about this man, and he is a great example of the holiness and righteousness God called us to in Bellingham. The atmosphere was dynamic and beautiful, because God was pulling people out of their sins and making them new creations.

As Christians, we are freed from the bondage to sin and death. God paid the ultimate price through Christ's death on the cross so that we would no longer be slaves to sin but alive in Christ. We now have no obligation to live according to our sinful desires.

Paul writes, "*For we know that our old self was crucified with him so that the body of sin might be done away with, that we should no longer be slaves to sin – because anyone who has died has been freed from sin*" (Romans 6:6-7 NIV 1984).

Later, Paul wrote, "*Therefore, dear brothers and sisters, you have no obligation to do what your sinful nature urges you to do. For if you live by its dictates, you will die. But if through the power of the Spirit you put to death the deeds of your sinful nature, you will live*" (Romans 8:12-13 NLT).

The young Canadian helicopter pilot felt this call to holiness. When he came to know Jesus (not just believe, but really *know* Jesus), it caused a profound change in his life. He left his sinful past behind, because he was no longer controlled by his sinful nature. Since he had the Holy Spirit living within him, he had the Spirit controlling him, not his sin. Even though he had to pay a price for his past sins that was just his physical body. His spirit had already been redeemed, and he brought that change with him into four years of prison, into a marriage, and later as an example to his daughters.

Some people think Christians are burdened down by rules. But the truth is, if you do not know Jesus, you are a slave. "*Don't you realize that you become the slave of whatever you choose to obey?*" Paul writes. "*You can be a slave to sin, which leads to death, or you can choose to obey God, which leads to righteous living*" (Romans 6:16 NLT).

Would you like to leave the slavery of your past behind? If you've chosen to obey your sinful nature your whole life, you can instead receive God's grace right now, in Jesus Christ. *"As for you, you were dead in your transgressions and sins, in which you used to live.... But because of his great love for us, God, who is rich in mercy, made us alive with Christ even when we were dead in transgressions – it is by grace you have been saved"* (Ephesians 2:1,4-5 NIV 1984).

But what about Christians who still sin, you may wonder. Those who truly know Jesus and are not just going through the motions have left this behind, as sons and daughters of God. I believe the ones still locked in lifestyles of ongoing, habitual sin have not discovered the freedom Jesus has to offer. Some have held onto those parts of their pasts that they like and enjoy.

Paul tells us, *"You, my brothers, were called to be free. But do not use your freedom to indulge the sinful nature; rather, serve one another in love"* (Galatians 5:13 NIV 1984).

Instead of indulging in sin, *"Delight yourself in the LORD, and he will give you the desires of your heart"* (Psalm 37:4 NIV 1984).

Have you held onto any parts of your sinful past? If so, you have not fully experienced the freedom Christ came to give you. Habitual sin can leave marks on our flesh, like that man's four years in prison, but Jesus died to set your spirit free from bondage to sin and death. Are you living like it?

CHAPTER 24:

NEVER GRADUATE FROM LEARNING

The church just kept growing, and eventually we simply could not remain in the funeral home. It was time for the church of the living dead to move.

We started looking for some land to build on, but the first try didn't go so well. I started draining the water from a very small pond on the land we bought, but we were stopped because there was a kind of frog that needed the pond we were draining to build our church. We left the frog to his pond and tried another piece of property. This was also a struggle, with many setbacks and difficulties. Then the same man of God who owned the offices we were renting came up with an idea. The offices were located on five acres, and he asked us to build the building on them and he'd lease it to us at an unbelievable price. So we started!

Finally, we were ready to pour the concrete for the sanctuary. After all the difficulties, I really wanted to just get this done without more delays, but a rainstorm was forecast. The contractor told me that if it rained, he was planning on taking his crew to Yakima on the eastern side of the Cascades for the winter. If he did that, we wouldn't get the concrete poured. This was now November, and we needed to be in the building by February 22.

With my staff standing there behind me, I told the contractor, "Let me tell you this: No matter what it does anywhere else in Washington, it will not rain a drop of rain on this piece of ground tomorrow. So you get those concrete trucks here, and you pour that thing tomorrow!"

Trouble was brewing on my staff, which I'll get to shortly, and one of them angrily said to me, "Who do you think you are? You're not God!"

"No," I replied, "I'm not God. God is God. But it is not going to rain on this piece of property tomorrow!"

But the words I said to the contractor had come up from my spirit and were from God. What I had told the contractor was a prophecy from the Lord: it was not going to rain. I believed that it was God's will for us to be in that new building, and I was going to stand on that resolutely and believe that God would see that it happened. My job was to go along with Him.

This was about faith: I believed God, not the weatherman.

We lived about four miles from the property where we were building the church, and when I got up in the morning, we were already in a rainstorm. I hopped in my car and headed over to the property. I was so excited that I could hardly contain myself. I knew it would not be raining on the property, and I could not wait to see it. About a half mile away from the property, I looked up into a clear blue patch of sky! All around, black—not grey or dark, but *black*—storm clouds hung low and dumped rain, but over our land was a circle of blue sky.

It was a miracle, the blessings of our Lord, and it went on *all day long!*

A string of concrete trucks came in, pouring and pouring their loads, and I just stood there on our property and praised the name of the Lord Jesus the Christ.

"This is not about our concrete," I told anyone who would listen, "this is about the glory of God and the souls of people."

It wasn't about my prophetic words coming true; it certainly wasn't about me. This was about a church being established that would change people's lives and would draw men and women to Christ Jesus. For that to happen like it was supposed to, we needed a bigger building. And for that to happen, we needed that concrete to get poured. And so God saw it through.

All through the day, a hole of blue sky brightened the construction site, while all around us a sea of dark storm clouds raged. A news crew came out, but I really don't remember what I said.

They were done with the concrete by about 3:00 in the afternoon. I was standing there when the contractor came up to me and said, "I just don't know how to say this, but you can tell 'Him'"—and here he sheepishly pointed his finger up at the sky—"that it's okay if it starts raining now."

I just laughed, and I said, "It doesn't work that way, but sure, I will. I placed my left hand on the contractor's shoulder and lifted my right hand towards heaven, and then I said, "Father, You know how much You love this man. He says it's okay if it starts raining now."

And it began to rain.

We had struggled to cram 320 people in our old building. We had 450 the first Sunday in our new building! It was ridiculous. In fact, we soon had to go to two services, which I had always resisted doing. I remember sitting there and watching people in between services and wondering, "Father, how did You do this?"

The Lord definitely has a sense of humor, and He gave me great ideas for ways to shake people up by doing what they didn't expect. One of my favorite memories from Bellingham was when the feminists protested at our church.

This was in the late eighties, and the feminist movement had impacted the Church as well. I was doing some studies on what women are called to do in the modern Church, and I wanted to preach a message on it.

But I wanted to do something that would really wake people up, so months in advance I told everyone I was going to do an evening sermon called "What Good Are Women Anyway?" By now, my name was known in the community—for better or worse—and so when the evening came to preach that sermon, we were absolutely packed. Some were there really to hear a message; some were there to criticize. Outside the church, best of all, some people were there just to protest, including NOW, the National Organization of Women. Of course, they had no idea what I was going to say, but with a title like that, they simply had to protest on principle.

I was so stinking excited! I went out covertly among the protesters, and I asked, "Hey ladies, what's going on?"

They told me about "that chauvinist pig in there" saying all these things. I told them, "You know what I would do? I would go in there, and every time that guy says something stinky, shout him down!" They liked that idea.

I slipped back inside the church, and of course they found out it was me when I got up to preach. After my message, those six women stood up with their hands in the air clapping because they'd heard me affirm that God loves and honors women! That got us in the paper again.

Also, it was my honor to see my father come to Christ. My mom and dad had moved up to Bellingham to be near us, and one day my dad called me with less than a stellar attitude. I had some of his gunsmithing stuff in the trunk of my car, so when he got so verbally abusive and hung up on me, I called back and my mom answered the phone. I told my mom to tell him that if he didn't come get his stuff, it was going to end up in the dumpster. When I got off the phone, I turned to my staff and told them, "My dad is going to come here, and he will be polite to all of you. In fact, he's going to get saved today."

The same man on my staff who questioned me about the rain spouts off, "Who are you to know that?" He didn't believe that God would simply tell me this.

"I promise you, today he's going to get saved. God told me this is the day; it's over. I don't have to pray anymore, it's done." I told them I just wanted them to go out to their offices and praise God for my dad's salvation.

When my father got there, he was very polite to the secretary, but when he got into my office he started to swear at me. I put up my hand and said, "Dad, stop!" and he stopped. "I have a question for you," I said.

"Why are you so afraid of being loved?"

Sudden tears filled his eyes. "Gus," he said, "I want to know the Jesus you know." We knelt, and he made another wet spot on my chair with his tears. I'd never seen my father cry, and he was sixty-seven years old at the time. He rarely smiled, but as he got up, he had this grin on his face. "Gus," he said, "I wish this had happened forty years ago! I would've lived a lot better life, and I would've made a lot more people happy."

We didn't know it at the time, but my dad would later develop brain cancer and be gone within five years. However, from that time forward, he turned into a powerful evangelist! He led my cousins to Christ, as well as many of his friends. He just had this unspeakable joy, and it was so sharply contrasted with how he'd been before that it stood out to everyone.

God did many other amazing things in those years. I was on television at times, and I had a lot of interaction with politicians and the like. But it was exhausting, and though I didn't want to admit it, trouble was brewing on my staff. It was only a matter of time until it boiled over.

You may remember that the Lord told me I would never graduate with an academic degree and get that piece of paper from the organizations of men that we can think legitimizes us. But that didn't keep me from studying when I had the opportunity, because I just loved learning more.

While still in California, I had the chance to go to Talbot Theological Seminary to work on my master's of ministry. When I asked how I could do that when I'd never completed my bachelor's degree, I graduated with what was called a missions certificate. They told me that because of all the work I'd done, they wanted me to have access to graduate studies. I dived into my studies, taking yet more Greek and acing my courses. However, with one semester left before I would graduate with a master's degree, we decided to leave and we went to Bellingham.

When we'd been in Bellingham about five years, I got a call from Northwest Graduate School in Kirkland, and they offered to let me work on my doctorate—even though I'd never finished my bachelor's or master's! I had to do ten classes to get my doctorate, and I proceeded to ace nine of them. Kirkland was eighty miles away, so I had to drive down there for a week at a time. I loved it.

During this period, I met and became friends with Ray Stedman, who had mentored Chuck Swindoll and Luis Palau. It was an amazing, life-changing relationship to study under this great man of God. I was able to learn from him in class, but I also had the honor of having lunch periodically and mentoring under him.

I am the most educated man without a degree you can possibly imagine!

I tell you all of this not to impress you but to remind you that nothing from men can make you more legitimate in God's sight. A piece of paper doesn't verify you are called by God. It does not make you more approved in heaven. It also does not guarantee that you will get to know Him better, though you can learn a great deal.

No institution of man can substitute for the call of God. When He calls, you answer—whether you receive recognition from men and women or not. You go; you answer the call. He will equip you, but you must seek Him to know Him.

God did not let me finish these degrees because of what He had told me in the desert—my only boast all the days of my life would be Him. It has remained true to this day!

Remember, you can only get to *know God* by spending time together with Him. You can learn *about* Him through studies, and you can learn to do things such as become a better public speaker. Knowing God through time spent with Him and learning in an academic setting are both good, but they are not a substitute for one another.

I thought you might like to know that the contractor who poured our concrete came to know the Lord. You see, it was never about *concrete*; it was about the eternal souls of people. It was about *that man's* soul.

When I said it would not rain, I was not grandstanding for press, boasting of my own godliness, or manipulating the Lord for something I wanted. I simply spoke what I felt He told me to say, but I said it quickly, boldly, and without preamble because *I knew Him.* I've learned to know the Lord's voice, and when He told me something, I was able to confidently speak it out.

How could I do that? How could I say something so bold, something that seems so brash and even arrogant? My own staff members didn't understand it. The answer is that it isn't bold or arrogant when you're just repeating what God has told you to say. And you can only do that when you know God's voice.

Some people will read this and think I'm crazy because they don't really believe God speaks at all or any more because they have believed a lie that God is silent. Others will read it and wish they could do the same thing but doubt they could ever be so bold for God because they have believed a lie from the enemy that there is something special about others enabling them to hear. Others may have some quiet voice inside that whispers that such a walk with God is possible for them, too, but they need some encouragement.

Whichever you are, I want you to know something: You too can learn to hear God that surely and confidently. There is nothing special about me; I'm just a guy who has gotten to know Jesus. All humans can learn to hear the Lord, because He made us in His image with the ability to speak to and hear our Creator, but it is a capability we must cultivate with practice.

You can learn to hear Him! Because when we do, it brings glory to His name.

When God held back the rain, it brought Him glory. It was not about me; it's never about us. It brought the Lord joy to show His miraculous power for the sake of that contractor and his crew and all the people who would worship the Lord in our church because our concrete got poured before winter. This entire thing was about God, His Kingdom, and the souls of the people He wanted to save.

Jesus tells us, "*Seek first the kingdom of God and His righteousness, and all these things shall be added to you*" (Matthew 6:33). In Psalm 37:4 we read, "*Take delight in the Lord, and he will give you your heart's desires*" (NLT).

This is important because it sets our priorities on God. It isn't about us. It is not about us prophesying, doing miracles, or counting the numbers "we've" led to Christ. When we make it about *us*, it's called "*pride*." When we make it about Him, it's called "humility." God lifts up the humble, but He opposes the proud, and if you want to operate in His gifts and miracles, it's vital to be on the right side of that equation.

We are to seek Him first, and we are to put our delight in the Lord—not in what He does for us or through us. When we make Him our delight, He is free to give us the desires of our heart.

So, what is your delight in? Is it in gratifying yourself? Your reputation, your ministry? If so, you're in for a surprise some day, because the Lord is a jealous God. If your delight is in your entertainment, your vocation, your family, or anything else, you are missing an amazing opportunity to be His disciple and learn straight from the Lord (see Luke 14:26).

My delight is in our Lord, and therefore I have the joy in the souls of men and women being redeemed from sin and death and coming to a saving knowledge of Jesus. So, it was the Lord's delight to hold back the rain for a few hours, which was the desire of my heart for His glory and for the souls of men.

The glory and power of God were on display that day, and when you synchronize the desires of your heart with the desires of His heart, you too will see His glory displayed on the earth.

CHAPTER 25:

ISRAEL AND ETHIOPIA

I had asked the board of elders of our church for permission to go to the Institute of Holy Land Studies in Israel. The church was now five years old, with four pastoral staff and an attendance of about 800. I felt I needed a break that would also refresh me in the depths of my soul. The Institute offered a study in the Old Testament, which was just what my wife and I had in mind. We had lots of homework to do before we got there, but we were very excited to do this together, and we would be living in old Jerusalem. Wow!

However, on the day we were to leave, my mom had a heart attack while I was preaching a Sunday service! She began to go grey right before my eyes as I was about to finish my message. We got some doctors forward, called an ambulance, and got her to the hospital. I was definitely not going to Israel now, I thought.

However, the doctors convinced us she was in good hands and that we should go anyway, and my mom also encouraged us to go. After a lot of prayer and soul-searching, we decided to keep our travel plans, and we headed to Israel.

Our flight landed in Tel Aviv, and then we had to take a bus to Jerusalem. Then, we had the privilege of walking three-quarters of a mile from our bus stop to the Institute of the Holy Land Studies where we were staying. Unfortunately, we found we'd overpacked. The bags were so heavy I could only carry one at time, and Karen couldn't even carry one, so I had to make two trips for our luggage.

We got our room assignment, and it was up at the top of the old Jerusalem wall, which made for a great view but also an additional ninety-seven uneven steps I had to carry each bag. The showers, restrooms, and the mess hall were downstairs. I will tell you this; when we left twenty-three days later, we were finely tuned physically from taking those stairs so many times a day! Both of us could fly up and down those stairs by the end. From the top of the wall we could look out over the entire valley of Gahanna.

On our first day as it was becoming evening, I was on top of that wall, looking out over the Valley of Gahanna. Then I began to hear sounds from below—voices. It sounded like a choir warming up. Then, instruments began warming up as an orchestra would do.

This tall black man came out from his room and joined me on top of the wall. I greeted him, and from his accent I could tell he wasn't an American, though he spoke good English.

"I am Werku Golle," he told me. I introduced myself and asked where he was from. "I am from Ethiopia," he answered.

"Ethiopia," I said. "I have never known anyone from there. Are you a eunuch?" I asked.

He laughed. "No," he replied. "I have five children." He would later have two more, too!

"Do you know what they're doing down there?" I asked him. He didn't know either. Soon Karen joined us as we sat on the top of the old Jerusalem wall listening to voices and musical instruments tuning up. Then suddenly it happened: On our first day and evening in Israel, the Jerusalem Philharmonic Orchestra and Choir played and sang Handel's *Messiah*. We were overwhelmed with joy and tears.

Over the next three weeks, we went all over Israel, seeing and learning where Joshua and the Israelites walked and established themselves. We studied and saw where the kings of Israel ruled and lived. We walked down many of the paths of the Old Testament prophets, and in our last days there we walked where Jesus the Christ our Lord walked. It was a life-changing time for both Karen and me.

Werku became a dear friend. Werku had been at Bible College in the United States when the communists took over Ethiopia. He felt God called him home, so he returned home, and he was providing spiritual leadership for his people when the communists put all the elders of the church there into prison. Then, after they put the elders into prison, they put Werku into the prison. They were not going to put Werku into prison the same way they did the elders. What they did with him was to dig a hole in the ground in the middle of the prison, and that is where they put Werku. They put a piece of tin over the hole and gave him a pot in which to use as a restroom. Werku's wife, Hallelujah, came each day to feed him.

He was in that hole thirteen months, and the only thing he ever said about that time was, "It was a wonderful time with our Lord."

In prison, the guards were told to beat the elders because they had been preaching Jesus. Then the elders were told that if they would renounce Jesus and promise not to speak of Him, they would let them go home.

"I cannot deny my Savior," they replied. So the beatings and imprisonment went on.

However, during this time in prison, the elders led many of the guards to Christ, one by one! Eventually the communists sent the church elders two hundred miles away to another prison, and they didn't tell their families what they'd done. But after many months, the communists concluded that these elders only did good for their communities and let them all go home. In fact, the communists looked up to Werku and the elders and gave them land in which to start a place to teach and worship. It was after these days that Werku was able to come to Israel where we met.

We always did big missions conferences at our church, and while our church only supported five or six missionaries, we liked to really focus on them and provide for them.

I had invited Werku to join our conference, and it was so holy that our church fell in love with him. After our conference, Werku invited Karen and me to join him in Ethiopia. We had to get special shots and a visa, and the state department sent me a letter that I shouldn't go because they could not guarantee our safety in the country and if something happened they could not get us out of Ethiopia. I sent them a letter back that I understood they could not rescue us but that it was okay—I was bringing my wife with me.

We could not travel directly to Ethiopia. We had to fly into Kenya, and there a missionary we knew picked us up and drove us up through the Great Rift Valley. It was the biggest zoo I'd ever seen, with giraffes and zebras and wildebeests everywhere! Our guide had us walk down this path to see some hippos, but he told us to be careful of lions. I wanted to know what I was to do if I saw one; how do you "be careful" of lions?

We made it down to an overwatch safely and looked out at the hippos. They were enormous! Little did I know that hippos kill more visitors to Africa than lions every year. Thankfully, these were busy swimming—one even went upside down, with his four feet sticking up in the air!—it was awesome!

We headed on, and our stop for the night was a hotel in a very small town near the Masai. It was a very little hotel, and when we saw the kitchen, it was the filthiest thing you've ever seen in your life. We sat down to eat our meal anyway, but Karen was so tired she literally fell asleep and dropped her face right into her food!

As they showed us to our room, they told us, "Make sure you keep your door closed all night because of the wild animals and snakes." I thought that sounded like godly wisdom. However, as we got to the room, I looked at the bottom of the door and noticed a three-inch gap between the door and the floor. Apparently only the really large snakes couldn't get in! However, we were so tired, we didn't even think about it.

We had to fly into Ethiopia on Kenya Airways, which Werku told us not to fly on. However, it was the only way for us to get to Ethiopia at the time. We got on board our jet, and when they started the engine, the cowling blew off! There was just a bare jet engine hanging below the wing, so we had to get off. Eight or ten hours in the very rough airport later, they brought in another jet. It was *old*. The carpeting was gone, and the overhead bins were all broken and just hanging. The seats were ripped and torn. It was a real act of faith just to stay on board, hoping and praying that their mechanical maintenance was better than the way they'd taken care of the inside of the plane!

We landed in Addis Ababa about midnight and found out the airport was closed. They let us off the dilapidated plane out on the runway; it just stopped, and we got off as soon as they got a stairway to it. When we got into the very small terminal, a communist soldier demanded our passports. We showed them to him, but then to our great shock, he *kept them*. He told us we would get them sometime in the days ahead.

We were now in a communist country with no papers.

Werku was there to meet us, but he was on the other side of this glass wall and couldn't get to us until we got our luggage and went through customs. I had brought ten guitars and two suitcases, and none of them were coming through the luggage carrousel.

After waiting for what seemed like hours, I hopped onto the moving luggage belt as it moved out of the terminal and back outside. Four soldiers were standing there outside, and when they saw me, they pointed their AK-47 assault rifles at my chest. That was really annoying! Without thinking about what I was doing, I slapped the guns right out of their hands and said, "Don't you do that to me!"

Another guy came up behind me and stuck his rifle in my back, and then they shoved me into this van. The other four soldiers picked up their AKs and got in the van after me. They shut the door and drove off.

I had no idea where they were taking me. To prison? To their army base? I started sizing them up; after all, I fought in Vietnam and I just did not like communists.

But then the van stopped, they slid the van door open, and I saw we were near the plane. They'd taken me out to the airplane! They opened a big cargo door on the plane, turned on some lights, and there were my guitars and suitcases. In fact, the four soldiers proceeded to help me unload the luggage into the van.

They took me back to the terminal, and when we got there, I shook their hands with my right hand and put my left hand over our right hands. I didn't know it, but shaking hands like that in Ethiopia meant that you were honoring them more than yourself. As I unknowingly honored them, these communist soldiers were blessing me.

I loaded the ten guitars and two suitcases onto the luggage belt and then hopped on it myself and road it back into the inside of the terminal. Karen and Werku were so happy to see me, but the other passengers were all looking at me expectantly, too.

"Where's my stuff?" they asked.

But I didn't have answers for them; I hadn't seen any other luggage on the plane—just our guitars and suitcases. Wherever the other luggage items went, ours were seemingly protected, so I thanked God for protecting me and our gear, and then I joined Werku and Karen as we headed out.

The next morning we headed out for Dilla, which was about 260 miles south of Addis Ababa. In those days, it was a long rough ride, but Werku had a new Toyota Land Cruiser, which really helped. When we finally arrived in Dilla we got a very warm reception. People had been waiting for us for hours, and when we pulled in, there was a banquet waiting in our honor. It was good food—normal food. And when we'd eaten, they brought out another course: Ethiopian food! To make us feel welcome, they had made American-style food for us, but now we got to try their local dishes. And through it all, in those days they served warm Pepsi, which was a great way to honor your guests. Since there is no refrigeration, you must drink it warm, so we drank more Pepsi than we ever had in our lives and were grateful for it.

Werku had me speak five times a day, two hours at a time! And we had to drive hours at a time to get to each location where I would be preaching. The roads were so rough! And though Werku had a great Toyota Land Cruiser, you were just beaten up and so dirty by the time you got where you were going!

That entire trip was amazing—we were overwhelmed to think we were in Africa. By the end of our two weeks, I wasn't feeling well and got really sick. I found out when I got back to the States that I had a bad case of mononucleosis. But it was incredible. God was moving, and He was establishing a lifelong friendship between Werku and myself. You never know when God is creating a divine connection that could change lives forever.

Perhaps you have wondered why you ended up in a certain place at a certain time—maybe somewhere not on your agenda and where you would never like to be. We never want to get our plans derailed by flat tires, hospital visits, or long lines at Starbucks. However, I have found that if we are open and watching for what God is doing, we will often find something He wants us to do while we're waiting.

Remember, if you are not looking for something, you will never find it. However, if you are looking for what God is doing, you will find

Him at work in small ways. Meeting Werku was one of those ways; our paths crossed, but we were both open and watching for what God can do through an interaction.

You may not want to be in the hospital waiting room, but what would happen if you looked around and saw who God might want you to speak with? What if your time there is not in vain? What if He needs you to speak to someone, encourage someone, or give them a word from Him in due season?

Divine connections are out there, waiting to be made, and I encourage you to look for them every day. God is at work; keep an eye open for His construction signs, because you never know when He has a task that is perfectly suited for you.

"For I know the plans I have for you," declares the LORD, "plans to prosper you and not to harm you, plans to give you hope and a future. Then you will call on me and come and pray to me, and I will listen to you. You will seek me and find me when you seek me with all your heart" (Jeremiah 29:11–13 NIV).

CHAPTER 26:

MY DAYS IN THE PIT OF DESPAIR

As I have alluded to, as time went on it became apparent that not all was well with my staff and within the inner workings of the Evangelical Free Church of Bellingham leadership. I had gathered a collection of people I liked, and I saw great potential in their lives. They needed a second chance in their ministry. Karen later told me, the biggest problem I had was that I wanted to help everyone who had somehow struggled or failed in ministry. I thought I could encourage them and give them assurance, restoring them to the position God had called them to.

Unfortunately, that meant that I had a lot of hurting and bruised people on my staff. Few were on the same page with me. It all worked well when I had the time to really nurture and mentor these individuals whom I loved and felt were also my friends. But, as I became overly busy with all the other ministry opportunities, like nineteen conferences a year; I was sometimes on television or radio, and I was also teaching at universities and seminaries. The stress began to take its toll. Tension began to build, and undercurrents of dissatisfaction and dissent began to grow just beneath (and sometimes not even that far) the surface.

Sometimes the interaction of my staff and some of the elders—the conversations they had in our meetings, for instance—made me very angry. They would argue over what I thought were the stupidest things, issues which were not about the Kingdom of God but were petty and political and rooted in this earth. I would get so angry, I would get silent, but then the energy had to go somewhere. I would sometimes just drop to the floor and do a hundred pushups so that I could send that energy somewhere other than yelling at them! I thought I was being gracious and handling it well, but as you can imagine it was not received well.

Understand, at this point in my life, I was still a former Marine, was still very disciplined, and was still forthright and learning to be overwhelmed by God's grace in the emotions of my life! I was learning to speak the truth in greater love, but I was still very plainly spoken and blunt, and I had little patience for foolishness. I told everyone that I was Gentle Ben, the titular character from a black-and-white era television show about a boy and his pet bear. It was only after I'd said that a lot that one of my staff mentioned that Gentle Ben was still a grizzly bear! I thought I was very loving, but as I look back today, it was a tough love. Sometimes people no doubt felt that when I was done loving them that they had been punched in the face!

Certain members of my staff became members of an underground resistance against me. The elders put one of my staff on probation three separate times, but those measures did not help him self-correct. I taught at many different conferences each year, and every time I went away, I came back to find that there were problems with the staff and the board of elders. No matter how many staff retreats we did, nothing seemed to bring these guys onto the same page with me in our view for the church, how the Lord works, or a few other things. The dissention really took on momentum, however, when I went to Israel and Ethiopia.

Eventually, in 1992, three staff members and three elders at the church, who had been apparently meeting for about ten months to figure out how to remove me, acted. Karen and I had been in Arizona interviewing a man of God about becoming our worship pastor, but when we got back, I was asked to meet with the elders. I thought it was going to be about the worship pastor we'd talked to, but instead two of the top members of my staff and some of the elders and the superintendent of the district were there to confront me.

"Before you say anything," they said, "know that we want you to resign immediately. If you resign, we'll let you leave in peace and keep your reputation. If not, we will do everything in our power to destroy your reputation." The superintendent told me I was completely unqualified to be in the ministry and that I was unfit and needed to be removed.

They said that I had the sin of anger, the sin of pride, and the sin of the appearance of wealth. So, they were making their move; I could leave quietly, or I could make it a fight.

When I asked them about the anger, they cited a time I'd yelled at our young worship pastor, who had stood up to argue with me in our staff meeting. He had indeed made me mad; he was extremely disrespectful to me even though I was old enough to be his father, and I did not respond to him with grace. Regarding pride, they cited the time I had said it wouldn't rain and the way I had projected numbers for the growth of the church—both of which I'd been right about because they weren't coming from me but from God. However, these people saw those statements as arrogance, not a living faith that is sure and certain.

Honestly, I knew that I could have trouble with anger. I was still a passionate person, but I was also quick to repent and had made great progress in grace since my days after Vietnam. And because these staff members obviously didn't share my belief that God can speak to us, I also can understand how they would think it arrogant for me to make statements on His behalf. I don't agree with them theologically, but I can see how they might find that arrogant.

However, the "sin of the appearance of wealth" complaint was a surprise. For years, I had paid members of my staff more than I paid myself at the church. I had brought in elders for the church to help make balanced decisions and to provide accountability and oversight to church issues, including financial ones. So, when they made this accusation, I was a little stunned. For years, every single one of the pastors on staff had a larger salary than I did. The elders just a year and a half before all this took place increased my salary to be just above the staffs'. But the sin of the appearance of wealth, I thought, what kind of sin is that? They said because I had bought a new car and was building a new house it appeared to them as sin. All I could say was, "Wow."

You may remember that after we moved to Bellingham, the Lord provided financially for the church in ways that made it seem like we had a lot of money. We were able to do things with the church and for the Lord, and He provided the money for outreaches and ministries and many other things. However, Karen and I did not benefit from that money personally; it just flowed through the church. We would have an idea or a leading from God, and we would step out to do that outreach or program, and the money would simply come. It flowed through; it didn't stay.

So, while I could recognize I needed to act with more grace and not give place to anger, and while I could understand that if you don't think the Lord speaks it seems arrogant to speak for Him, I could not understand why they thought I had a "sin" of the "appearance of wealth."

"This is not going to happen," I told them. "I am not going anywhere." I chose to stay—I would not go down silently while they tried to take what the Lord had built. I told them the glory of God and the name of Jesus the Christ were at stake.

I called the president of our denomination, and they sent out a consultant, a mediator who was a Christian psychologist who would interview everyone and try to help the situation. The president of the denomination told me this was a good, godly man and that I could trust him. I did; we became friends.

The consultant interviewed everyone, and he came back to me and said, "You're completely different than everyone on the staff says." Two of them had told him I was arrogant, unteachable, and all these other things. "I don't see that in you," he told me.

The consultant prescribed that Karen and I take eight or ten weeks off, during which time he was going to mentor the staff and try to work through their problems. We had a meeting with the staff and elders, where he told them this, and everyone agreed. He said that if we shook his hand, we were making a binding agreement. We all shook his hand, signifying our agreement to go forward with his recommendations.

Karen and I abided by it. We went down to the counseling center in Fresno, California, where we were to rest, be renewed, and be refreshed. We weren't to talk to anyone about the church, and that was very difficult for me, because for all these years, ministry had been my lifeblood. I had poured everything I had into that church, and it was my every thought.

However, three days after we left, the firebrands on the staff had a meeting of their own, which we didn't know about until much later. There they decided that they didn't need to abide by what the consultant had said because he in their view was a "liberal." During all the weeks Karen and I were being renewed and refreshed, thinking the consultant was helping them work through their problems, they were in fact moving against us.

In the end, the dissenters started their own church. They spread many lies, and they obviously were still very wounded people to say and do the things they did.

As I mentioned, I had surrounded myself with people I really liked, but they were hurting people, and when I could no longer give them as much time as they wanted, they became angry. It was sad, and I was not without fault in these things, but it never should have gotten to the place it did, and they never should have pursued it as personally as they did. They set out to destroy my character.

Karen and I were gone for ten weeks, and when we returned, one of the guys on staff, whom I loved, was doing the preaching. The church still had a thousand people, even without those who had gone to the new church the dissenters on my staff had started. But one of the remaining elders and the member of my staff who was preaching had decided that, since we'd been gone ten weeks and he had been preaching, that he should now be the senior pastor. I told him no, so he left with some more people to start another new church.

The contractor who was building our house was part of the people who left initially. He transferred a large sum of money from our account, supposedly to finish our house, but he never finished the job. Nor did he pay the subcontractors. So, we returned to Bellingham to find the church split, our house unfinished, the subcontractors suing us, and no money in the bank. In addition, wild, untrue rumors were roaring around the area.

I tried to work toward restoration or at least understanding, including going to the office of the first church split, but they did not want to talk to me. I was brokenhearted. We had started the church in Bellingham when I was thirty-six, and now at forty-five, it was crumbling.

Then my dad started dealing with brain cancer during this time—rumors flew that God was killing him because of my sins—and while he was a terrific witness during his treatment, it resulted in dementia. Also, he couldn't beat the cancer, and it simply was eating him up. It was difficult to see him suffer, but his heart was so changed that he even preached to the people as they did his treatments!

Throughout my life, my dad had never told me he loved me until the last few years of his life. After he got saved, he told me that frequently. Eventually, the cancer consumed his body, and Dad went into a coma. The doctors told me to continually talk to him because even though he was in a coma and could not respond, he could hear.

On what would turn out to be Dad's last day here on earth, I had been with him all day. As I was leaving the hospital, I told the doctors to please call if anything happened. I no sooner got home and they called. I went and picked up my mom and went to the hospital. When we got there, Dad was still in a coma lying on his side. Mom was at his back, and I went to the front and held Dad's hand. Then I said, "Dad, I just want you to know I'm here. I love you."

My father had been in a coma for almost four days, but his eyes fluttered open, and he sat up. "Gus," he suddenly said, "I want you to know something. I love you, son!" And then he sagged down and simply stopped breathing.

He was gone.

Four months later, my mother was still having kidney dialysis, and somehow on that day during dialysis her potassium went low, she fell asleep, and her heart stopped beating. I came to pick her up, and she was lying on the floor. They tried to resuscitate her, but while they got her heart started, she was no longer there. Three days with no brain activity later, we turned off the machines that were keeping her alive. After a time, she suddenly took this breath and seemed to sit up. She seemed to lose all her age and looked like she was twenty years old again, and then she too was gone. Almost exactly four months after I lost my father, my mother passed as well.

I had thought we'd be in Bellingham forever, and because the church had constantly grown week after week, I thought that God's work would simply continue to expand. Now, church politics and personality conflicts would break my connection with the work God had been doing at the Evangelical Free Church of Bellingham.

I had no idea that something like this could happen. My entire life seemed to be collapsing before my eyes. I felt like Job. First the church, then my home and money, then my father's cancer and death, and then my mother's sudden death. I was in a really deep, dark place—a place I've never been before.

In that season of my life, which God was allowing, I was about to learn something that I could not have known any other way. Faith is sure and certain because of the real fact that God's Word is true, factual, and filled with life. I was entering a season where my Lord would overwhelm me with His grace, kindness, and love. I was about to learn the reality of God's eternal Breath.

Paul writes,

"And we know that in all things God works for the good of those who love him, who have been called according to his purpose. For those God foreknew he also predestined to be conformed to the likeness of his Son, that he might be the firstborn among many brothers. And those he predestined, he also called, those he called, he also justified, those he justified, he also glorified" (Romans 8:28–30 NIV 1984).

I was about to learn in real time through great heartache the magnificence and awe of our Lord. "*Though the fig tree does not bud and there are no grapes on the vines, though the olive crop fails and the fields produce no food, though there are no sheep in the pen and no cattle in the stalls, yet I will rejoice in the LORD, I will be joyful in God my Savior. The Sovereign LORD is my strength...*" (Habakkuk 3:17–19 NIV).

CHAPTER 27:

WHERE IN THE WORLD IS POST FALLS

After the repeated hammer blows I took the final years we were in Bellingham, I was mentally and physically and emotionally exhausted. I didn't want to leave the church in chaos, but we no longer wanted to stay there where so many things had blown up, both in the church and in our family.

We began to intensely pray about where we should go and what we should do, and we began to get the impression that God was drawing us to Idaho. It's gorgeous country, and we thought we would take the opportunity of a move, after ten years of ministry in Bellingham, to simply recuperate. I had no intention of starting a church or ministering; we just needed a break.

We'd managed to get our house finished. When the subcontractors had sued me, I was able to produce meticulous records of how I'd paid the contractor who ran off with our money, so we were now able to sell our finished house and walk away with more money in our pockets than we'd ever had before. We would be able to use that money to make a new start.

In Idaho, I felt like I could breathe again. I didn't want to go back into the ministry or start churches; I actually thought about buying a Harley Davidson dealership. I was still going to live for Christ, but I didn't feel like I had it in me to be a pastor anymore. The pain was way past being exhausted.

So, we moved out to Coeur d'Alene Lake, where we rented an old cabin for three months. I bought a motorcycle, obviously a Harley Davidson, and we just rested. We rode the bike, took in the scenery, and just spent time at the cabin doing nothing. It was here that I really learned the true value of rest.

However, after we'd been in the cabin a few months, the Lord woke me up around 3:00 in the morning. I got up and went outside, kneeling down on the deck, and looking out over the moon-lit lake.

"What is it, Father?" I prayed.

I'd had time to rest and heal, and the Lord's timing is always perfect. He said, "I want you to start a church in Post Falls." Post Falls is now a bedroom community for both Coeur d'Alene and Spokane, but at the time there wasn't much there.

"Okay, Father," I answered after a time. "But this time, You build the building. I don't want to build buildings anymore. I'll preach Your Word, but I don't want to do small groups, disciple, or counsel. I just want to preach Your Word." I felt like I could do that; the rest was too intimate, too close. When people you've discipled and been close to turn against you, it just hurts too much. I didn't want to do that anymore.

I told Karen, of course, but I also told a friend, Doug, whom I'd known from my time doing conferences. We used to joke around, and I'd say that if he ever "got right with God"—he was right with God, it was just a joke—that he should come to Bellingham, and he'd say that if I got right with God, I should come over the mountains. So now I was thinking of starting a church "on the other side of the mountains," so I met with him to tell him what God had said.

"Post Falls?" he said. "Nobody is in Post Falls!"

Doug was a youth pastor at the time, and wanted to always be a blessing. "I'll start it with you," he finally said.

"I'm not going to pay you anything," I told him frankly.

That got his attention. "How do I know if God wants me to do this with you?" he asked.

"Put yourself in a place where if God doesn't answer your prayers, you're dead. It's then that you experience His blessings and will," I told him.

He smiled. "You're pulling the right string, but you've got the wrong yo-yo," he told me.

We went back and forth about where we should start the church, but I was sure God had said Post Falls. "Where do you want to start it?" Doug asked, meaning a location.

"I don't know," I answered. "I'm not looking. God's going to have to do it, because I'm not building a building!"

"Well, I'll find us a building, but I want to look other places, too." I finally agreed, and he started looking for buildings. For months, he looked and looked, but he found nothing.

One day I had an appointment and was in Post Falls when Karen and I went down the wrong road. And because we were on the wrong road, we looked up and saw something we hadn't noticed before: a church building with a sign that said, "For Sale or Lease."

We called the realtor, and he said he could come show it to us. Karen and I looked it over with the realtor, and it was pretty rough. Sheetrock was on the floor, the roof had a leak, and it was really overgrown and disused. But none of these were problems I couldn't fix; after all, I'd been a roofer.

I saw potential—an opportunity.

"Could we use this?" I asked the realtor.

"When?"

"Sunday."

He laughed. I was asking this on a Thursday. "Really?" I nodded. "What time?"

"Ten?"

He thought about it. "How 'bout this…I can have an open house on Sunday. You and I can come early, and we'll sweep the sheetrock out of the way."

And that's exactly what we did. We didn't advertise or say a thing other than telling friends and so forth. We had one lady who agreed to play the keyboard, and on October 3, 1994, we held our first service after sweeping the sheetrock out of the way.

Sixty-seven people showed up!

I was very annoyed. God had told me to start this, but I didn't actually want it to go anywhere; I didn't want it to ask anything of me. I was obeying, but I felt like I just didn't have it in me to do the big, growing ministry thing again.

The denomination that owned the building told me they wanted $2,000 a month for the building, but because most new churches fail, they wanted $2,500 a month. That didn't make any sense to me, but we had the money, and I honestly still wasn't sure if we wanted it to make it or not! So we agreed.

We couldn't use the building the following Sunday, so we met in a room on the Spokane river and had seventy people show up. I don't even know how they found out where to go! They just came. However, the week after we were back in our dilapidated building, cleaning it up to host Sunday services. We made one room into an office, and we got ready to have church.

One day Doug told us excitedly, "I did it!"

"Did what?" I asked.

"I quit."

I said, "What!? I can't pay you!"

Doug smiled as he said, "I know. But you said that if I got to a place where if God didn't answer my prayers, I'm dead, that I'd experience God's blessings. I want to be there. I want to know God that way!"

Little did I know that we were *both* in that place.

This was the first time that God did not provide the money monthly for the church. The way He provided the money was the proceeds from selling our house: we funded the church for a year, because offerings weren't really coming in. But people kept coming in and getting saved! I had said I didn't want to meet with them one-on-one, but I did, and the church kept growing.

We started in October of 1994, and in August the next year, Doug and I got our first check—$1,000 for each of us. We had no money left in our account by this point, and it was at that very point of being in a position where if God didn't come through we were dead that the money began to flow in from tithes and offerings.

We named the church "His Place" because my staff at the church in Bellingham had forgotten that the church was God's place, not ours.

God called me into action when I didn't have it in me to start something new on my own. Without Him doing the work, I never would have started a new church, because emotionally, I was still in a very dark place. I was preaching fine, but inside I was in shambles.

Few knew how depressed I was. I told my brother-in-law, Jim, my doctor who'd married my sister. Before, when people told me they were "depressed," I thought it was all hogwash. I thought there was no such thing as debilitating, major depression. I thought they were "choosing" depression or something.

I learned differently.

"If you have a broken arm, Gus, can God heal it?" Jim asked.

"Sure." I replied.

"What does He normally do?" he asked.

I replied, "Well, He sends you to the doctor, who puts a cast on it."

"Gus, this is the same thing. The chemicals in your brain are empty. If they're a bank account, you're bankrupt! There are five things that bring on major stress and send people in major depression, and you've experienced all five! You lost your father and mother, your job, your house, and your money in a matter of months. You're being slandered, so you've even lost your reputation. Of course, you're completely depressed. I think you should see a Christian psychiatrist."

I agreed to do it, and I proceeded to take a bunch of tests with the psychiatrist. He told me that if anyone had even three of the major negative life events I'd dealt with, they would likely be in trouble. I had all five, and he told me he was surprised that I was still able to function at all. He prescribed an anti-depressant, and after taking it for three weeks, I woke up one morning telling Karen, "I'm back!"

I hadn't even known how far gone I was until I got some help getting back. I used that helping hand for six months, and then the psychiatrist began weaning me off it. I didn't crash back down without it, so we knew that I had navigated the darkest hours.

The church kept growing, and God progressively restored my love for the Church and ministry. It took time for me to heal enough to return to the call of God on my life, and it took rest, a forward vision, and accepting help.

In the end, it provided me a unique opportunity. I do not believe that God caused any of this—no kingdom can survive being at war within itself—but I know without a doubt that He can work all things together for our good.

David wrote, *"He lifted me out of the pit of despair, out of the mud and the mire. He set my feet on solid ground and steadied me as I walked along"* (Psalm 40:2 NLT). That describes exactly what the Lord did for me.

Are you in the middle of a dark time? Do you feel trapped in a pit of despair, like your feet are sunk down into the sucking mud? If so, lift your eyes to the hills, for your help comes from the Lord (see Psalm 121:1-2). As surely as He made a way out for me, He will make a way out for you, too.

I think it's important to note that though I received physical rest—which I cannot promote enough as a means of healing—and help from people and medication when it was needed, the source of all help is the Lord. He dispenses these things that help us and is our ultimate source for everything we need. Seek Him first, do what He tells you to do, and watch as He will walk through the darkest valleys with you and lead you out the other side.

CHAPTER 28

EMBRACE YOUR OPPORTUNITIES

In my darkness, I learned something intimately: God comforts us in our suffering, but He in turn uses us to comfort others. Paul puts it this way:

> *"All praise to God, the Father of our Lord Jesus Christ. God is our merciful Father and the source of all comfort. He comforts us in all our troubles so that we can comfort others. When they are troubled, we will be able to give them the same comfort God has given us. For the more we suffer for Christ, the more God will shower us with his comfort through Christ"* (2 Corinthians 1:3-5 NLT).

Out of the opportunity of my own grief and pain, God began to develop something new in me that has allowed me to minister to pastors and others who are burned out and hurting. God taught me the incredible value of rest and recuperation and the boundlessness of His unending grace, and He used those lessons as a way of equipping me to minister His overwhelming grace to people in difficult trials.

He also taught me the power of "opportunity." You have perhaps noticed that I've used this word freely to describe difficult times, because I believe every challenge is an opportunity for God. They are opportunities to discover who we really are in Christ, and it is in these hard times that we see the extent of His grace's power. No matter if it's persecution, sickness, loss, or tragedy, it is an opportunity for God to change lives—yours and those around you.

The devil wants you to think there's nothing more permanent than your temporary situation, but the truth is that our troubles are only momentary, and they are not comparable to the great joy awaiting us.

Later in 2 Corinthians it says, "*For our present troubles are small and won't last very long. Yet they produce for us a glory that vastly outweighs them and will last forever!*" (2 Corinthians 4:17 NLT). In another place, Peter tells us to be glad, for there is wonderful joy ahead of us, even though we endure troubles for a little while (see 1 Peter 1:6).

Your current "opportunity" will not leave you the way it found you. So, you have a choice to make: You can see the obstacle as one that is taking you out. Or you can humbly and meekly see it as a chance for God to produce glory in and through you.

The choice is yours.

God gave me an opportunity to recover in Idaho, but some part of me knew it wasn't permanent or long term—it was a parenthesis in my life, a time of healing and rest that He was using to help me recover. From the get-go, I designed His Place so that one day I could step away and it would go on. I made Doug a senior pastor—not co-pastor, but a senior pastor with me. He and I had very different gifts, and while I was the visionary, he was the one who had a knack for making things work. My idea was to groom and bless him to replace me by mentoring him and developing him.

Five and a half years after launching His Place, I felt like God called us elsewhere. The church was healthy and growing, and Doug had grown immensely as well. We had the chance to move back to California, and I knew Karen had always loved it there. We would head to San Diego, together with Dan, a worship pastor who'd been with us at His Place.

We visited San Diego and met with the superintendent five times before we committed, but then we sold our house and moved down there…only to get a rude awakening that once again we'd moved under false assumptions. Apparently the superintendent who'd flown us down was making decisions out ahead of his board, and they weren't in agreement. Perhaps something had changed since our initial talks, and when I got there they said there was no position, no salary, no nothing.

My focus was on ensuring that Dan and his family were provided for (we had a little money saved up, the board did end up giving us a very small salary, and His Place was supporting us like missionaries), but it was just a matter of time until we would leave California once again. Dan got a full-time job, and the attempts we made to start something in San Diego fell flat, though we did lead some people to the Lord.

Ten months after moving, we got a call from a friend in Idaho, Charlie, and he invited us to come back up to Idaho and stay with them in the apartment above their four-car garage. He urged me for a time and I turned him down, but eventually we agreed. We stayed with them for about four months, and it was awesome, but then Karen fell and broke her ankle badly. It required surgery and metal screws, and I had to carry her up the stairs to our apartment above the garage. So, when we got a call from another superintendent asking us to come to Kansas, we thought it was time for a change and entertained the idea enough to go out there.

The superintendent came out to us in Idaho a few times, and I went to different conferences in the Midwest district, getting to know the people. I learned they were really friendly, and eventually we moved to Kansas City. It was nice, because all our stuff had been in storage in San Diego, and we'd just been subsisting in the apartment over the garage. We liked having our own place with our own stuff again, and our new neighbors in Kansas welcomed us very warmly.

I wasn't pastoring a church. I was going to conferences and speaking at different churches. I met the pastors and sat in their Sunday services, and then I helped in the ways I could. One of the pastors I visited was Jim Anderson in Overland Park, Kansas. He was a great guy, and we liked a lot of the same things. However, something was immediately obvious to me about Jim. I could see clearly because my own dark time had left me with new insight into the struggles others faced.

I attended a Sunday service, and Jim wanted to have breakfast the next morning. He asked me, "So, what did you think of my preaching?"

I told him, "I've never heard you preach."

"What do you mean?" he asked. "You were there Sunday."

"I heard a tired man talk," I answered. "Jim, you're tired. You need some rest." I knew the look from personal experience—he wasn't in sin or doing anything wrong, he was just exhausted. If he'd run two marathons back-to-back, there would be no shame in being tired. So, too, there was no shame that Jim was tired; he needed help.

But when they asked me if I would help, I told them "no." That was my default answer now. I used to say, "I'll pray about it," but at that point in my life, I just said "no."

They persisted, and the superintendent who'd brought us to Kansas wanted me to help them, so I called and told them what it would take. They had to agree to lay aside their agenda for six months. Jim, the pastor, needed a six-month sabbatical, and for three of those months I'd mentor him and minister to him, but for the rest of the time he was simply to rest. I'd work with his staff and elders, and they would accept it with a smile on their faces, and after six months Jim would return and resume his duties.

They agreed, so Jim and I began to meet three times a week. I mentored him on the Eternal Breath of God, encouraging him and

232

urging him deeper in the Lord, just pouring into him to restore him. I also met with the people on staff and the elders.

During this time, the church grew by about one hundred people, and everyone was doing well. But Jim was concerned that I may try to take over the church, so I told him, "I do not want to take over any church. I want you to pastor your church as a refreshed man of God."

I arranged a big surprise celebration for him when he returned, and everyone was so excited—including Jim. He was nervous like a first-time pastor again. Would they want him back? Did they like me better than him? He wasn't sure. So, I went out of the way to make sure he felt incredibly welcomed. When he and his wife walked into the back of the church, everyone jumped up and started yelling and clapping in their excitement to have their pastor back.

It was an incredible experience to see this man of God refreshed and ready to come back and do the work God had called him to do. And in this ministry of refreshment to him, I found another level in my calling—ministering to hurting, exhausted pastors so they could be more effective in their ministry. This would be the genesis of Overwhelmed by Grace.

Perhaps you know what it feels like to be simply exhausted and worn out. If so, you're one of the ones for whom I wrote this book, a story of my own "opportunities" that hopefully encourages you. It is my hope that in reading it you can experience God's grace and rest, which we do through meekness.

In his book *Pursuit of God*, A.W. Tozer writes, "Jesus calls us to his rest, and meekness is His method. The meek man cares not at all who is greater than he, for he has long ago decided that the esteem of the world is not worth the effort." Tozer cites Jesus' sermon on the mount where He tells us, *"Blessed are the meek, for they shall inherit the earth"* (Matthew 5:5). Only much later, Tozer explains, does Jesus tell us what this meekness means and how it connects to rest? Jesus says, *"Take my yoke upon you, and learn of me; for I am meek and lowly in heart: and ye shall find rest unto your souls. For my yoke is easy, and my burden is light"* (Matthew 11:29-30 KJV).

So often we make service to God about *us*—about what *we* can do for Him. We make it about us. But the person who embraces meekness, which is strength under control, understands that on our own we can do nothing, but with Christ, we can do all things because whatever strength we have comes from God's endless supply.

Even the Apostle Paul faced this challenge. This great man who wrote much of the New Testament tells us of his own opportunity: a "thorn in his flesh" given to him to keep him from becoming proud. He writes, *"Concerning this thing I pleaded with the Lord three times that it might depart from me. And He said to me, 'My grace is sufficient for you, for My strength is made perfect in weakness.' Therefore most gladly I will rather boast in my infirmities, that the power of Christ may rest upon me"* (2 Corinthians 12:8-9).

Accepting this weakness, this "thorn," in order to receive God's grace is only possible when we are meek and humble in heart. The proud resist God's help; the meek understand they cannot do without His grace as their supply.

You do not know this to be true when things are going well; you only learn that His grace is sufficient and His strength works best in weakness when you are weak and exhausted. When life's trials and opportunities wear you down or reduce you to your foundation, you see what it's made of. If your foundation is built on your own strength and abilities, it will come crashing down. But if your foundation is built on the Rock of Jesus Christ, the wind and rains may beat against you, though all else comes crashing down around you, your foundation will hold firm.

Paul explains it like this:

"We now have this light shining in our hearts, but we ourselves are like fragile clay jars containing this great treasure. This makes it clear that our great power is from God, not from ourselves. We are pressed on every side by troubles, but we are not crushed. We are perplexed, but not driven to despair. We are hunted down, but never abandoned by God. We get knocked down, but we are not destroyed. Through suffering, our bodies continue to share in the death of Jesus so that the life of Jesus may also be seen in our bodies" (2 Corinthians 4:7-10 NLT).

The next time troubles press you on every side, you're confused, you're persecuted, and you're simply exhausted, with Paul you can gladly boast not in your own strength, but in God's, because His power is made manifest when we rely on His grace.

My own dark time let me see clearly when others were exhausted and in difficult times, and because I had been comforted, I had comfort to offer them. That is the opportunity I gave to Jim, the pastor in Kansas—the same opportunity I've had the chance to give other pastors as part of the ministry of Overwhelmed by Grace—the comfort of God's grace and rest. And it is a vital part of this book that you learn your trials and struggles are just opportunities to receive God's grace and strength. No matter what you're going through right now, whether it be health challenges, financial difficulties, relational problems, or anything else, His grace is sufficient for you. When you humble yourself, you will find that His yoke is easy and His burden is light, and in meekly relying on His grace, you will find rest for your soul.

CHAPTER 29

THE CHURCH OF MY DREAMS WAS A NIGHTMARE

Ever since coming back from Ethiopia in 1990, I had stayed connected to Werku, and I had gone back to Ethiopia every other year. Werku became one of my best friends since we met in the city of our great King, Jerusalem. When I first spoke to their leadership, I preached to about 150 people in a little mud room. In the following year, we helped them financially to build a new building that would hold up to 3,000 people. When I came back, I got to preach to the church leaders of Ethiopia in this new building on the church compound.

In the wake of moving to Kansas, I felt like I had no real commission from the Lord. We were just looking for what He wanted us to do, so while I was in Ethiopia, it was a time of ministry to them but also intense prayer as Karen and I sought what God wanted us to do next. While I was there, I fasted the first three and a half days, drinking only water as I preached at the leadership conference.

During this time, I had a dream. In my dream, I was in Tucson, Arizona (which I'd never actually been to), and I went up this long driveway to a church with a really tall cross. I saw what the front doors looked like as I passed through them, and then I went up to the pulpit and began to preach. I was preaching about the Kingdom of God, and it was incredibly real. I saw all these people in the church, and to my right, one wall of the church was all glass, which allowed you to look at some spectacular mountains. At the end of my message, I gave this invitation to come to receive the Kingdom of God, and the glass wall swung open. Suddenly thousands of people from Tucson were there, bowing their knees to the Lord.

When I woke up it was 3:00 in the morning, but I wrote down as much as I could remember about what I had preached while it was still fresh in my mind. I knew that this was the answer to our prayers: this was the direction I had wanted from God. The Kingdom of God was moving, and we would see what Tucson had to do with it.

It was the last day of the conference, and I was to preach from 10:00 till noon. I delivered the message from my dream, and as I did so, the Holy Spirit just came down on that place! It was amazing, and even the six guys I'd brought with me from the States could only sit in amazement with their mouths hanging open.

"You don't know what you just did," Doug, from Idaho, told me.

"It's not me," I told him. "That's the Holy Spirit." Then I told him about the dream and the message I had preached. I knew somehow that had something to do with our next step.

I shared that dream with Charlie Worley, a great friend, and who was our church planter minister for the Kansas district. Charlie, with great joy, shared my dream and the results of my preaching in Ethiopia with the superintendent who brought us to Kansas. His name is Bill, and he is a good friend of mine to this very day, but he was hurt and somehow offended. So, he came to our home and started yelling at me in my own house in front of my wife, under the assumption that I was not going to honor the five-year agreement we'd made with him. In fact, he said he'd help me get to Tucson—by firing me!

He gave me two weeks, and—typical for us—we had no money even to buy airline tickets to Arizona to look and see what God might have planned. However, God—typical for Him—was ready to provide. My brother-in-law, the doctor from Bellingham, called, and I told him about the dream and my opportunity of being fired. He immediately said, "I'll help you. I'll call you back in a few minutes."

He bought us two round-trip tickets to Phoenix and put us up in a five-star resort for ten days, as well as renting us a convertible Camaro while we were in Arizona! His generosity was incredible, but behind him was God, making it all possible. Like I said, though we've often had no money, God has taken care of us like we were wealthy. I would never have booked a five-star hotel or a convertible, but God, our Provider, treated us lavishly again, thanks to my brother-in-law's generosity. Less than twenty-four hours after getting fired, God had provided for our trip to Arizona.

We put a "For Sale by Owner" sign in the front yard, and two days later we were on a plane for Arizona. Somehow this guy Dave, who'd been a missionary to Venezuela, heard we were coming—I have no idea how—but he'd heard me at one of the conferences I'd done years ago. He claimed it changed his life. So, he wanted to meet with us, and when I asked where, he gave the address for a church in Tucson.

As soon as we turned into the driveway of this church, I slammed on the brakes. It was the same long driveway of my dream, the same tall cross, the same front doors. I finally drove the rest of the way up, and we parked and went in. Even the glass wall overlooking the mountains and the pulpit were *exactly* as they had been in my dream. The only slight disappointment was that the glass wall didn't swing open.

A guy came out, the worship leader, who was from Australia. I asked, "Who's the pastor here?"

"We don't have one. We're looking for one. You want the job?"

I was stunned, but my reflexive answer was "no" at this point. I just was there to meet Dave, I thought. We met Dave and just got acquainted. While we were in the church building, we felt a spirit of tension and did not know where it was coming from because we knew no one there.

We headed back to Phoenix and our hotel, and we visited a church there pastored by Bob Fox. He had started the church ten years earlier. He was thinking of leaving the church because he felt like he'd taken it as far as he could. But I told him, "No you haven't! You're just exhausted." When I met Bob, I knew I had met a man after the heart of our Lord. I told him our story, my dream, and about getting fired and asked him if we were to move to Arizona where he would recommend as a place to move to.

Bob suggested a town called Gilbert, so we drove around and found a cute little house for rent. But the owners wouldn't hold it for us, even though they liked us because we didn't know when (or if) we were coming. We told them we completely understand and then said if your house is the house our Lord has planned for us, it will still be available when and if we come.

While we were standing there talking to them, a realtor in Kansas called me from the front yard of our house there. She had a client who really liked our house, and they later bought it at the asking price!

We went back to the resort having found the church, sold our house, and picked out a house to rent. In the month it took to finalize everything, they still hadn't rented the house—in fact, no one had even come to see it. We moved out to Arizona without knowing what we were going to do, with no income, and only our trust in God.

The next thing I knew, the church from my dream called and asked if I'd like to come preach. They'd been a church of nine hundred, but they had been reduced to just 140 people, many of whom were meaner than snakes (in Jesus' name). Pulling into the parking lot, I felt this oppressive heaviness. Something was very wrong with this church. Something was so wrong with this church that while in the parking lot I said to Karen, "If I did not have to preach here today, we would leave right now." We got out of our car, walked towards the front doors of the church, which were still closed, and as I opened the door a man looked at me and said, "You're late."

I told him the time I had been told, and he said, "We have changed the times." Then he threw at me a headset to put on, and I walked into the men's room.

"Father," I said as I got ready in the men's room, "it's time for You and me to do something." I asked Karen to be praying as I got up to preach.

I put my Bible on the pulpit—the same one I'd seen in my dream—and I looked out over the scattered congregation in their too-large auditorium. "Men and women of God," I greeted them, "thank you for having me here, but I've got to tell you something before we get started. There's something desperately wrong with this church. I pulled into your parking lot, and I felt something so evil and so dark, I parked as far away from your front door as I could. If I didn't have to speak here today, I would not be here. I would have left!" And with that, I opened God's Eternal Breath.

I was fully expecting them to mob me after the service for my frank honesty, but instead they asked me to consider being their pastor! I said no, and I told them they couldn't pay me enough to come pastor there. But I'd agreed to preach three weekends, so I was back the next two weeks and preached. They asked me again to consider coming as their pastor. I said no! So they asked would I fill out an application. I said no! Then they asked would you at least pray about it and I said *No!*

I was meeting with Bob Fox and his staff in Phoenix, and they honestly reminded me of my staff in Bellingham. I was trying to bring refreshment and fan their flames back to life, and at first it seemed like nothing was happening. But suddenly they all just got lit on fire for

God, Bob seemed to be so refreshed in our Lord. He had been thinking of leaving, but suddenly he realized he wasn't going anywhere because the fire of the Lord had sprung back to life in him and his staff.

Bob talked me into interviewing to be the district superintendent, and when I talked with the selection committee, they seemed very hostile. Some of them knew people from my staff in Bellingham and had heard the lies and rumors they spread, so as Bob and I drove back together, I had little expectation I would want to be their superintendent or that they'd want me. Bob, however, was convinced I was the right one for the job. And sure enough, to my incredibly great surprise, they unanimously asked me to come!

I inherited the thirty-nine churches of the Southwest Border District of the Evangelical Free Church of America, which included Los Vegas, Arizona, New Mexico, and El Paso, Texas. Many of them were not healthy, and a handful were outright dying. As I began to visit them, I realized that the pastors and their wives weren't healthy either; they were exhausted, drained, and worn down.

So, I planned to bring all the pastors and their wives to the Sheraton Hotel in Tucson. We put on a conference to re-fan the flame of our Lord in their lives, their marriages, and their ministries. I found the district had enough money to pay for all our pastors and wives, so they could come for free. And our Lord overwhelmed them with His presence during those days.

The one church in my district I didn't want to visit was the one I'd seen in my dream. I didn't want anything to do with them! It had been eighteen months since I'd first preached there, and they still didn't have a pastor. They'd turned down sixty-two applications.

They asked me to come preach again, and I reluctantly agreed. Afterward, they asked again if I'd consider filling out an application to be their pastor, and again I turned them down. However, they persisted, and I finally agreed to meet with them.

As I explained my philosophy of ministry, I told them that churches that became institutionalized made it a business rather than a relationship. When he heard this, the chairman of the elders jumped up and said, "That's our problem, we're already institutionalized. We're not relational anymore. What would you do to help us?"

I told them they'd have to set aside their rigid programs and critical spirit, as well as many other things. "If we did all this," they asked, "would you come?"

"No."

But they wouldn't let it go. Finally, I said, "If I were to come, everyone would have to agree to the philosophy of ministry, and I want the resignations of everyone on staff. I'll pick my own staff."

I thought this would break the deal, but to my surprise, they agreed! They voted, and they asked me to come. My first day, I walked into the bare little office to see the resignations of three of the four staff members waiting for me. The one who hadn't was the worship leader. Within a month he started talking stink, and the elders fired him on the spot.

I was now the pastor of the church from my dream, but there was still so much wrong with it, it was more of a nightmare. I was also the superintendent of the district, and I had several dying or unhealthy churches that needed a move of God to refresh and rejuvenate them. They needed to be overwhelmed by God's grace, because they had tried and failed to do it on their own. Exhausted and worn out from operating on their own strength, they desperately needed a touch from God. So did the church where I became the pastor.

I'll be honest: I didn't want that job. I didn't want to go into that church that was so pressed down under a dark cloud. But God had given me that dream for a reason, and He'd equipped me with an understanding of what it means to need refreshment, rest, and restoration. I had received God's grace, and now He was calling on me to give it out to hurting people.

This is often how God does it. He equips those He calls, and if you've been through great trial and adversity and found your strength in the Lord, then you often have unique insight into that kind of "opportunity." You've been there and done that, and you are wiser because of it. Now, you can in turn help someone else. Having been hurt, burned out, and depressed, I knew the signs. And I knew what God could do to help people who were afflicted like this.

Isaiah prophesied, "'*No weapon formed against you shall prosper, and every tongue which rises against you in judgment you shall condemn. This is the heritage of the servants of the Lord, and their righteousness is from Me,' says the Lord*" (Isaiah 54:17).

God has a way of prospering you with the very weapons the enemy forms against you. Instead of letting it destroy you, He has a way of taking them captive to His own good plans for your life and turning them back against our enemy, the devil. Like David who picked up Goliath's own sword and used it to cut off his head, on the other side of our challenges are opportunities to take the fight to the enemy using the very thing he intended to destroy us. That is part of why I say that trials are just opportunities.

Right now, I want you to think of the greatest difficulties you face and then imagine what life can be like in five, ten, or twenty years when God has worked them for your good. He can do it, and He does it regularly if we will respond to Him humbly. Nothing is impossible for you when God is with you, and He will turn your enemy's weapon of destruction to your good, so encourage yourself in the Lord and look to see His plan for your life turn even these things to your good.

CHAPTER 30:

LIVING OVERWHELMED BY GRACE

God often gives us dreams—not to show us where the easy path is, but to prepare us for His work of grace. The work He gave me in Tucson at the church of my dream proved to be difficult, but it was work I was called to do. And it furthered the gestation of the ministry that was the culmination of everything God put into my life, Overwhelmed by Grace.

The church grew from about 140 to about 500, and I brought some great people onto the staff to help me. Together with Dave, who'd been a missionary to Spanish-speaking nations, we did conferences in Mexico City as well as outreaches closer to home. Jim came on as Pastor of Student Ministries, and in him I saw my successor.

I committed to five years at First Evangelical Free Church of Tucson, but I learned that I was the newest of six pastors who had come to lead the church only to have the leaders turn against them. When I learned of the fate of the other five pastors, I knew God wanted to minister healing and grace to them. I invited them, including the one who'd led the building campaign for our current facility (only to be fired and then legally restrained from ever setting foot in the church he'd built), to come for a banquet in their honor. We went all out, and every pastor since the founding pastor came and enjoyed steak and lobster. I had a huge book made and set it on the platform, and within it was the name of each pastor and his wife, the years they were there, and the things God had accomplished through them.

I called each one up separately to thank them and show them their page in the book. When the former pastor—the one who'd never gotten to step foot on the property before—came up, he was sobbing uncontrollably. None of these men were released with honor and respect, and so as we honored them as a congregation, I could see that God was bringing His healing touch and grace to the situation. It was overwhelming!

"We are here to bring healing to the Body of Christ," I told everyone. "It is time to repent for treating these men without honor. You need to repent, because the way they were released was dishonoring to the Lord."

They did, and there was hardly a dry eye in the house.

But some people seem to fall back right into their old thinking and ruts. I had only been there about two years when they tried to get rid of me, too! However, unlike the five pastors who came before me, this time the roughly forty people who'd held the power before lacked the support. These were influential people in town…at one time. They'd been there thirty plus years. However, now they were older, and the new people who had come since I arrived were not swayed. At one morning service, about forty older people stood up as one and left during the service. And the church was much healthier for it.

God did tremendous work in that church and in me while I was there, and I believe that this was simply a part of the ministry of restoration that God had called me to—a lifelong call that He had been developing slowly within me. I was on assignment, and as the five-year mark drew closer, I knew my time there was coming to an end.

About two years before I was to leave, I had already begun mentoring Jim to succeed me. At that point, there was no way the leadership would've accepted him. However, a year before I was to leave, most of them had come around, and at the five-year mark, the congregation had a 100 percent vote confirming Jim as their new senior pastor and the budget—the first time the church had voted 100 percent on anything, ever!

At my final message, I put a washbasin and a towel embroidered with Jim's name and the date, which I had put on the platform where no one could see them. I preached the Word of God to Jim, ordaining him as the new pastor. Then I asked Jim to come onto the platform and had him sit in a chair while I took off his shoes and socks and washed his feet while talking to him about being a man of God.

"This is a holy calling," I told him. "You're called after the heart of God. You're not called to the ministry; you're called to God so that this ministry can live."

After I'd washed his feet, I prayed and leaned my forehead onto his feet. As I prayed God's blessing on Jim, I could feel the Lord's pleasure, and when I stood up and looked out at the congregation, it seemed as if every man, woman, boy, and girl was weeping.

"The baton has been passed," I told them. And then I stepped down as pastor and into full time with what was still just glimmer in my Father's eye.

During that time we were praying about what we were to do next and for Karen's dad to come to the Lord, I had another amazing dream. This time, I did not see a church; instead, I saw the throne room of God. My attempts to describe it always fall so short, but I could *see* the glory of God like it was a tangible thing. The train of His robe filled the temple, and somehow it was *alive*. But it is not a robe; it is His *glory*, and it moved of its own. Its colors are like nothing you've ever seen on this earth—colors that are alive. In fact, everything about God is alive, so full of life and abundance that it is staggering, for there is no death or darkness in His Kingdom.

I was standing in the throne room, and I was wearing white. My arms were lifted in praise, and I could see my hands, and they were no longer old. Somehow, music and songs were pouring from my innermost being, and I was weightless because there was *no sin*. Here on earth we do not realize how heavy we are weighted down by our own sin, but there I was completely clean and sinless, and I was filled with unspeakable joy. All I did was look at the glory of the Lord as the train of His robe moved in its glory and songs and worship poured out of me to Him.

While I was singing, I heard the Lord speak to me. "Gus, you have always been overwhelmed by Me. What I am about to do in you, I want you to call 'Overwhelmed by Grace.'"

"Father, it sounds good to me!" I replied, and then—*bam!*—I was back in my bed, waking up. However, I didn't want to be back. I wanted to stay there!

It was 4:30 in the morning, and I woke Karen up, and I did my best to describe what I'd just seen. Again, my words fall so short, but what stayed with me was that God was doing something new—something overwhelming in me.

I told a select few people about what God had showed me and Overwhelmed by Grace, and I was blessed that some of the strong leaders around me caught the vision and helped me with details. Ron, a dear friend of mine, helped secure a website, and three other men of God who are my friends paid to have a lawyer establish Overwhelmed by Grace Ministry as a 501c3 non-profit ministry. I literally had to do nothing, because God blessed me with such amazing supporters.

A guy who rented vacation houses for a week at a time approached us that ours was in an ideal position, so rather than selling our house— we didn't know if we were going anywhere yet or not—we simply rented it out. Instead, we stayed in our fifth-wheel trailer and prepared to travel. We've always loved to travel, and over the years we drove our Ford camper van for over 200,000 miles, and now we had a beautiful new Ford diesel truck and fifth wheel.

Being freed up of our commitments at the church was a real breath of fresh air for me. I was up one morning meeting with our Lord, and He brought to my mind Mike Garman. I felt we were to go and see him and his wife Sandy. I asked our leadership team from Overwhelmed by Grace if we could and they sent us off with a blessing. Mike was in high school when I first met him, and I saw him commit his whole life to our Lord then; his mom was the woman who told me to get out of Allan's church in the Los Angeles area so many years ago. Mike now pastored First Baptist Church in Paso Robles, and he really wanted us to come visit.

I noticed immediately that Mike was exhausted. His wife Sandy, too, was tired and a little bit angry. He'd been there fourteen or fifteen years, and he simply needed a break. After I saw the state Mike was in, we had a meeting with his elders—some of whom would grow into great friends—where I explained that it wasn't that Mike was in sin, he was just exhausted. They agreed to send him on an eight-week break if I would come and preach for him.

I hadn't thought of doing this until they asked, but I immediately saw this is what God had been preparing for us. This was the ministry of restoration that God had called me to in action—my first outreach doing Overwhelmed by Grace full time. Over those eight weeks, I preached for Mike, but I also met with him every other day to just pour into him, and I met with his staff and the elders every week as well.

Mike stayed there in Paso Robles, and I got him into road biking to shed some weight and get healthier. While I was there, the church went from about 300 to about 400, it went from being in the red financially to in the black, and God simply came in a restoring way to both the church and to Mike. When he came back, he was refreshed, and so was his staff, the leadership—and his congregation.

God had given the ministry of Overwhelmed by Grace its first success story, but it would not be its last. We began to travel to different churches, ministering to pastors much as we did to Mike and his church. We also attended conferences, and I discipled in men's groups such as Band of Brothers back in Tucson.

We eventually sold our house and bought a motorhome—a Newmar Mountain Air, which was a nice model and a lifelong dream for both of us—and simply traveled from place to place doing whatever God told us to do. The relationships I'd built over the years at conferences and through other connections now became some of the very people who needed a breath of fresh air and a rest. Most of the churches we visited were within the Evangelical Free denomination, but soon even pastors and churches who didn't know me personally were asking us to come.

We spent time in San Antonio and Austin, Texas, Nebraska, the Dakotas, and Idaho in addition to our home turf of California, Arizona, and New Mexico. The pastor in Nebraska may have been the first who didn't know me personally who asked us to come; and the first time I preached there, it was like God just came down and breathed on us all. The atmosphere of the church changed just like that, and the pastor and his staff just got lit on fire for God.

It was a great time, and God provided for our every need each step of the way. We didn't ask for a set fee, so for instance Mike's church in Paso Robles wanted to pay me personally, but we told them to just give something to the ministry of Overwhelmed by Grace. Back in Tucson, some of the members of my board were to be raising money, but a couple of them were very well off and were just putting the money in themselves, which we didn't know at the time.

We have had teething pains, like any ministry, as the kinks got worked out, but every time I see a tired pastor or his staff reenergized and restored, I know we were doing the right thing. We loved the traveling, and we were doing the very core of what God had called us to so many years before—breathing the living Breath of God onto those whose flames were flickering. We had the privilege of seeing men and women in leadership earnestly seeking the Lord again.

This reminds me of a story by Charles Haddon Spurgeon. A young man came to him and asked Spurgeon if he would teach him how to preach like him. Spurgeon said, "Take the Word of God and go spend time alone with Him until He sets your soul on fire, and they will come to watch you burn." There is no one like the Lord. I love Spurgeon's clarity.

That may be you—you may be worn out, exhausted, and flickering…even going out. It can feel like God has even abandoned you in a dry and weary land. But while all others may abandon you or let you down, the Lord never will—He will always act according to His character as a loving Father.

Prophesying of Jesus, Isaiah wrote, "*Look at my servant, whom I strengthen. He is my chosen one, who pleases me. I have put my Spirit upon him. He will bring justice to the nations…He will not crush the weakest reed or put out a flickering candle. He will bring justice to all who have been wronged. He will not falter or lose heart…*" (Isaiah 42:1, 3-4 NLT).

You too are that servant He will strengthen, and He has given all of us His Holy Spirit so that we may not falter or lose heart. Elsewhere Isaiah wrote, "*Even the youths shall faint and be weary, and the young men shall utterly fall: But they that wait upon the Lord shall renew their strength; they shall mount up with wings as eagles; they shall run, and not be weary; and they shall walk, and not faint*" (Isaiah 40:30-31 KJV).

His grace is sufficient for you, my friend (see 2 Corinthians 12:9). No matter what you're going through, how tired you are, or how dismal the outlook, His grace is enough for you. And the weaker you are, the better you'll be able to see His power at work in you, because it is only when we realize that we are powerless to do it in our own strength that we see Him and His grace come through.

In ancient agrarian times, oxen and horses performed farm work. They would put a shaped piece of wood on the shoulders of two oxen so they could pull together, and with one another's help, they would plough the field. Jesus tells us that His yoke is easy, and His burden is light, because whatever call God has placed upon your life, Jesus is yoked beside you, and He pulls far more than His own weight (see Matthew 11:30).

When you rely on the Lord to be your strength, He can show you the extent of His power at work within you, and you will see how He bears you up with wings like eagles so you do not grow weary and lose heart.

His grace is enough for whatever you need. In fact, it's overwhelming.

CHAPTER 31:

NO ONE LIKE THE LORD

The ministry of Overwhelmed by Grace has grown and developed over the years. Some of the details have changed, but the core of it is true to the call God has placed on my life—to minister His grace to people wherever we find them, even hurting, exhausted people. We've had the privilege to travel across the country and minister in a variety of ways, and looking back at the course of my life I can see how God was preparing me for this very thing.

I have had a blessed life, and I can now look back and see how God was drawing me to Himself. From childhood where I spoke to God in the beauty of His creation in Hawaii to experiencing the wind of the Spirit literally blowing my hair back in Oregon, I feel like I have known God all my days. Even when I did not want Him with me in the jungles of Vietnam, He never left my side. There is no one like the LORD! "*For I am convinced that neither death nor life, neither angels nor demons, neither the present nor the future, nor any powers, neither height nor depth, nor anything else in all creation, will be able to separate us from the love of God that is in Christ Jesus our Lord*" (Romans 8:38-39 NIV).

He put the faith within me to believe in Him.

What if there is a God? I have experienced Him and known Him intimately for most of my life, and without doubt I can say not only that there is a God but that He is good beyond measure.

Scripture is clear: "*Without faith it is impossible to please God, because anyone who comes to him must believe that he exists and that he rewards those who earnestly seek him*" (Hebrews 11:6 NIV). Philippians 2:13 tells us, "*For God is working in you, giving you the desire and the power to do what pleases him*" (NLT).

It pleases Him for us to know Him. He wants relationship with us and to give us His greatest gift: Himself.

The Psalmist wrote about his own desire to know God: "*As the deer pants for streams of water, so my soul pants for you, my God. My soul thirsts for God, for the living God...*" (Psalm 42:1-2 NIV). This is what it is to live overwhelmed by grace—it is a desire for intimacy with God that aches within us like a thirst in our souls. I know this feeling, and I pray that you do too.

But it is a choice. We must realize our desire is for God, and many people mistake this thirst for something else and pursue everything *except* God. Yet everything else is empty without Him. We yearn for Him within the very DNA of our beings, but all too often we chase things that are so empty.

We think learning will satisfy, but it just fills our minds with facts, and not always the truth. We think vocation will satisfy, but it just keeps us busy and urges us to spend ourselves climbing the ladder. We think sex will satisfy, but without Him as the source of love, it eventually leaves us empty and used. We can even search for our fulfillment in family, only to find that people grow up, leave home, and eventually die.

It echoes words of Solomon, the wisest man in the world, in Ecclesiastes when he writes, "'*Everything is meaningless,' says the Teacher, 'completely meaningless!*'" (Ecclesiastes 1:2 NLT). He spends an entire book illustrating the ways in which we foolishly chase after meaning and fail to find it without God.

I began this book by asking, "What if there is a God? Could there be anything greater than knowing Him? Could He possibly give you anything that was better than Himself—His presence with you every moment of every day?"

And over and over, I have seen people respond by saying, "I want to know the Jesus you know." They see Him in me: The answer is and has been in Jesus all along.

The answer is knowing Him.

David, Solomon's father, told him this answer long before Solomon first asked the question. David wrote, "*Delight yourself also in the Lord, and He shall give you the desires of your heart. Commit your way to the Lord, trust also in Him, and He shall bring it to pass*" (Psalms 37:4-5). Jesus would later confirm these words when He told us to seek the Kingdom of God first, above all else (see Matthew 6:33).

There is no need to exhaust ourselves seeking fulfillment everywhere else, for there is no one like the Lord. There is no substitute that can replace Him; there is nothing that can compare to Him.

No experience on this earth is a match for simply knowing Him intimately and personally and being overwhelmed by His grace. Whether this book has hopefully helped you come to know Him for the first time, or if you've read this because you are exhausted and need to get to know Him anew, the answer remains the same as it always has been: knowing Jesus.

It is my prayer that this story of a headstrong young Marine who came to Jesus and learned of His grace inspires you to want to know Him more deeply. The cry of my heart is for you to know Him—not about Him, but to *truly know Him*.

With Paul I can say that I have not already reached perfection in this but that I press on that I may lay hold on that which Christ Jesus has already given to me. I have not yet achieved, but I am determined to forget the failures of the past and keep my eyes fixed forward on completing the race that God has set before me (see Philippians 3:13-14 NLT). At times, I have been very tired in this journey, but God's overwhelming grace has enabled me to go on.

If you are tired, be encouraged. Every saint of history is urging us on, cheering us as we press toward the finish line. "*Therefore, since we are surrounded by such a huge crowd of witnesses to the life of faith, let us strip off every weight that slows us down, especially the sin that so easily trips us up. And let us run with endurance the race God has set before us. We do this by keeping our eyes on Jesus, the champion who initiates and perfects our faith*" (Hebrews 12:1 NLT).

If you already have a relationship with Jesus, but you're burned out, weighed down, tired, and worn down, my prayer is that you are encouraged by this, because I've been where you are. I pray you're able to throw off whatever holds you back from pursuing Him—knowing Him—with your whole heart.

You may think that failure or sin has disqualified you, but it is not true. I too have failed, sinned, and dropped the ball throughout my life. But God showed me a taste of His overwhelming grace in His throne room and gave me an experience with the weightlessness of being without sin.

There is no condemnation to those who are in Christ (see Romans 8:1). That means you. If your emotions condemn you and say you've failed, it's a lie, and it's not from God.

I declare you righteous—now and forever, not on my authority but by the power of Jesus Christ and the blood that He shed for you. God never condemns us, and it's His kindness that leads us to repentance and restoration (see Romans 2:4). He died once, and it was enough for anything you have ever done and will ever do. He didn't do it grudgingly; it was His good pleasure to make you right with Himself (see Ephesians 1:5).

"When we were utterly helpless, Christ came at just the right time and died for us sinners" (Romans 5:6 NLT). We were dead in our sins, but God's grace and forgiveness were so much greater than the sins that try to hold us in bondage! Adam's sin led to condemnation for the whole human race, but God's gracious, gift of His Son made us right with Him. God's wonderful gifts of grace and righteousness triumph over sin and death for all who will receive them. Sin once ruled over us, but God's overwhelming grace rules us instead, giving us right standing with God and eternal, abundant, unending life through Jesus Christ our Lord (see Romans 5:12-21).

If for one moment you simply take Him at His Word, just for a nanosecond, it will remake you forever. You will be lost to the kingdom of darkness, and you will be a powerful asset to the Kingdom of God. Nothing will be impossible, and no setback will ever again threaten to be a failure. You will see trials as opportunities and difficulty and persecution as privileges. You will walk in His righteousness, peace, and joy in the Holy Spirit.

Righteousness is the deliverance from our guilt and from the power of our own sin. It is integrity and life without hypocrisy. It is a goodness in the love of God that we experience and give to others. And God's righteousness produces His peace.

Peace has no condemnation in it or rudeness. It actually means "harmony." The definition of harmony is sympathetic vibrations in a natural harmonic series. For example, if you lift the lid of a piano, you will notice a lot of strings. Tap one of the heavy strings and watch what happens. You will visually see a natural harmonic series. Without touching any other strings, strings will begin to vibrate along with the one you touched.

That peace, that harmony, is now ours and we can vibrate in harmony with the Holy Spirit. God's peace brings a natural harmony between God and you and that will affect all relationships. His peace brings His joy.

Joy has no worry, stress, or anxiety with it. Joy is tension-free, for it comes from the Lord in the beauty of the Holy Spirit. Joy will encourage in some of the most difficult places. Here is God's desire for us: *"For the kingdom of God is not a matter of eating and drinking, but of righteousness, peace and joy in the Holy Spirit, because anyone who serves Christ in this way is pleasing To God and approved by men"* (Romans 14:17-18 NIV 1984).

When we have intimacy with God—not just knowledge of God, but intimacy with Him—we vibrate with the Holy Spirit to the tune of righteousness, peace, and joy.

If you have lost your song, lost your harmony, you can regain it. If you're lacking your sense of righteousness, peace, or joy, prayerfully go back over the events of your life and ask God where you lost it. Quit condemning yourself and feeling bad, and start spending time with Him so He can change your thinking back into harmony with His. Open your mouth and rejoice in the Lord! Give thanks to Him and watch what happens to your emotions as these things become your habit.

His desire is to restore you to Himself. His greatest desire is for you to want to know Him. And He can restore whatever has been lost between you in a moment when you stop going your way and repent.

Living a life that is overwhelmed by grace is a life in the Kingdom of God. It is loving the Lord your God with all your heart, all your soul, all your mind, and all your strength. You do not do this on your own power; you do it by the strength of His grace, which is sufficient for you.

Whether we are far from God and lost in sin, or if we are simply weary and losing heart, God's desire is the same for us: to know Him.

It is my desire for you, too—that you would want to know the Jesus I know.

There is nothing like Him. When you come to know Him, He will change everything about you—for the better. And when you have simply been weighted down by too many cares and burdens, He will bear you up. He will declare you righteous, He will give you His peace, and He will be your joy.

I leave you with this:

"Rejoice in the Lord always, I will say it again: Rejoice! …Do not be anxious about anything, but in everything, by prayer and petition, with thanksgiving, present your requests to God. And the peace of God, which transcends all understanding, will guard your hearts and your minds in Christ Jesus. Finally, brothers, whatever is true, whatever is noble, whatever is right, whatever is pure, whatever is lovely, whatever is admirable – if anything is excellent or praiseworthy – think about such things" (Philippians 4:4,6–8 NIV 1984).

There is no one like the Lord and His love for you!

AUTHOR CONTACT

If you would like to contact Gus Bess, find out more information, purchase books, or request him to speak, please contact:

Overwhelmed by Grace

179 Niblick Road
Suite 427
Paso Robles, CA 93446

520-400-6431

overwhelmedbygrace.com

Follow Gus!

facebook.com/overwhelmedbygrace

twitter.com/gusbess